D1192310

Priorities
in TZEDAKA
Higher forms of giving

Priorities

By Rabbi Moshe Goldberger

IN CONJUNCTION WITH NACHAS UNLIMITED

in TZEDAKA

Higher forms of giving

NACHAS UNLIMITED

Nachas Unlimited is a most unusual non-profit, tax deductible charitable organization. It was formed by a group of grandparents who wanted to share their *nachas* by helping other children.

It's a simple idea making a major impact. The beneficiaries are underprivileged, disadvantaged and abused children and their families in Israel and America, who are offered funds for medical needs, baby formula, clothing, cribs, layettes, and *britot*.

Nachas Unlimited further directs much-needed funds to child-related organizations that deal with crib death, abandonment, disabilities and illnesses that afflict infants and youngsters.

Nachas Unlimited has no payroll and all volunteers perform their activities *leshem mitzvah*. There are none so proud or as powerful as parents and grandparents who *shep nachas*. Now you can put that pride and power to work with your involvement and contributions to

Nachas Unlimited
22 Niles Place
Staten Island
New York 10314

OR FOR MORE INFORMATION VISIT US AT
WWW.NACHAS.ORG

CONTENTS

Acknowledgements

A work such as this is truly a collaborative effort on the part of many people. It is only fitting that we give *hakoras hatov* to the many individuals involved in the publication of this sefer. First, to Rabbi Moshe Goldberger for a brilliant rendering of a difficult subject. Next, to Milton Pfeiffer and Nachas Unlimited for suggesting and coordinating this project. Sincere thanks to all those *rabbanim* who read the manuscript, made suggestions, and gave their *haskomos* for the sefer. In particular, thanks to Rabbi Reuven Bulka for his work with the manuscript. We owe gratitude to all those who sponsored dedication pages, allowing for the publication of this *sefer*. Sincere thanks to Saul Feder and Mindi Fried for their readings of the manuscript, their suggestions and their encouragement. Finally, thanks go to the editor, Lydia R. Kraus, for her revision, editing and proofreading of the manuscript.

LETTERS OF APPROBATION

HASKOMOS

We wish to thank all those *rabban-im* in America, Canada and Israel who supported the undertaking of this *sefer*. We are indebted to them for their suggestions and additions. We are particularly thankful to them for the giving of their *haskomos* for its publication.

Rabbi Reuven Feinstein
131 Bloomingdale Road
Staten Island, NY 10309

הרב ראובן פיינשטיין
ראש הישיבה
ישיבה דסטעטן איילנד

Dear Rabbi Goldberger, עמו"ש

I very much enjoyed perusing the rough draft of the sefer you are planning to print regarding the Halachic priorities when giving tzedakah. Though in the footsteps of my esteemed father, Harav Hagaon R' Moshe Feinstein, זצ"ל, I can not write a Haskama on it, for in order to write a Haskama on practical Halacha, one must review each specific Halacha from its source to ensure its accuracy. Unfortunately, the constraints of time and public responsibility do not allow me the luxury of examining your work with such depth and detail.

However, the parts that I've read have given me much pleasure, and much credit must be given to the author and those who have prompted him to research and write this sefer, "מגלגלין זכות על ידי זכאי", for this timely topic is an extremely important one.

When one gives Tzedaka, he must ensure that he is giving because of <u>what</u> he knows, not just <u>who</u> he knows. To give just because this is the "in" organization that the popular crowd donates to causes the neglect of many important Tzedakos and creates a terrible environment in which people do not fulfill their communal and social responsibilities of tzedaka and chessed. It is a work such as this one which will hopefully begin to open the eyes of the community to realize that Tzedaka is a responsibility which must be managed with the same seriousness as one's personal finances. Tzedaka monies are not ours, per se, but rather money with which the Creator has bestowed upon us custodial responsibilities, to ensure that they are disseminated properly, following the Halachic guidelines of priority and responsibility.

The fact that this project has been undertaken by an individual as esteemed as R' Goldberger, י"נ, one of the distinguished alumni of our Yeshiva, whose many other Seforim attest to his knowledge and dedication, "חזקה אין חבר מוציא מתחת ידו דבר שאינו מתוקן", guarantee a finished product which can serve as a basic guideline to these Halachos, to empower each individual to know what and when to ask his Rabbinic authority and to open up our hearts and minds to this topic, which is one of the underlying fundamentals upon which the world rests (גמילות חסדים).

May Hashem grant you and your supporters the Siyata Dishmaya to see this project through to its fruition, "שלא יכשלו בדבר הלכה וישמחו בכם וכו'", and may He grant you the wisdom, health, and wealth to begin many other projects, to strengthen the dedication of Hashem's nation to Torah ideals, along with your families and their offspring, "עד ביאת הגואל בב"א"

RABBI DR. TZVI HERSH WEINREB
Executive Vice President

April 13, 2007

Rabbi Moshe Goldberger
POB 82
Staten Island, NY 10309

Dear Rabbi Goldberger:

Through the good offices of Mr. Milton Pfeifer, I was provided with an advance copy of your forthcoming book entitled "Priorities in Tzedakah – The Art of Giving." The topic of triage, or kedima in tzedakah giving has always been a very important one, and is particularly important in our times. Tsorchei amcha merubim, the needs of the Jewish community are many. But our resources are limited. It has become extremely important that our community learn to direct its tzedakah to the neediest and most deserving institutions first, and only later to other legitimate institutions. It certainly needs to learn to eliminate those causes which are not only not priorities, but are not legitimate at all.

Your Sefer provides an excellent framework to help individuals and congregations determine what their tzedakah giving priorities should be. The Torah expertise which you bring to bear on this topic is formidable, and admirable, and I congratulate you on that. But I also congratulate you for your common sense approach and for the quality of your presentation.

In these days when day school tuition weighs so heavily upon our young families, and when our basic institutions of education are struggling·so, it is important to emphasize to the community that such Torah institutions are indeed a priority. Other causes slide down to the bottom of the list when compared to the urgent needs of fundamental Jewish education for all Jews who seek it.

In my position as Executive Vice President of the Orthodox Union I hope to disseminate your work and see to it that it is read and considered seriously by a wide readership. I wish you hatzlacha on this endeavor and thank all of those who have supported you in publishing this vital work and in helping to guarantee that our tzedakah priorities be re-thought and re-allocated.

Respectfully,

Tzvi Hersh Weinreb

Rabbi Tzvi Hersh Weinreb, Ph.D.

THW:LB

March 29, 2007
10 Nisan 5767

Milton Pfeiffer, President
Nachas Unlimited
22 Niles Place
Staten Island, NY 10314

Dear Mr. Pfeiffer:

Shalom aleichem.

Thank you for sending me the manuscript "Priorities in Tzedakah: Higher Forms of
Giving," written by Rabbi Moshe Goldberger in conjunction with Nachas Unlimited, Inc.

I found the material to be informative, challenging, thought-provoking and most practical.
Any reader of the *sefer* will not only learn the philosophy behind the *mitzvah* of *tzedakah*,
they will learn how to give, what to give, when to give and, of course, the priorities of
giving. They will learn the benefits of giving and the joys of giving. They will learn that
tzedakah can be given with one's resources other than money. The reader will be able to
internalize the *mitzvah* of *tzedakah*, to make it a part of who they are.

Yasher koach for your efforts, *yasher koach* for caring for your fellow Jew. I wish you
continued *hatzlacha* in all your future endeavors.

Sincerely yours,

Rabbi Pesach Lerner
Executive Vice President

Legacy... Community... Family...

בית המדרש אהל יצחק
CONGREGATION OHEL YITZCHOK
137 - 58 70 Avenue
Kew Gardens Hills, New York 11367
(718) 261 - 7037

שאול אריאלי
רב

הנה הגיע לידי הספר „עדיפויות בצדקה" מכבד המחבר המפורסם הרה"ג ר' משה גולדבערגער שליט"א

אשר נטל על עצמו לברר וללבן את ענין מצוות צדקה לכל פרטיה.

בעברי על הספר, ראיתי הרבה עמל וגיעה שהשקיע הרהמ"ח בביאור שיטות וחידושים מרבותינו הראשונים

והאחרונים ז"ל, וערכן וסידרן בטוב טעם ואין ספק שחבור זה יהיה לתועלת הרבים.

והנני לברך את הרהמ"ח שימשיך לשקוד באהלה של תורה ויזכה לזכות הרבים בחיבורים בשאר מקצועות

התורה.

וע"ז באתי על החתום ביום ה' שבט תשס"ז פה קיו גארדנס הילס נא יארק

5 Shvat, 5767

I am privileged to receive a copy of "Tzedakah Preferences", compiled by Harav Hagaon Moshe Goldberger, Shlita. The esteemed author has undertaken the task of comprehensively researching and explicating the multifaceted Mitzvah of Tzdaka.

Upon reviewing the volume I was duly impressed by the efforts invested by the distinguished author in elucidating the spectrum of insights and rulings provided by the Early and Late rabbinic authorities, of blessed memory, and presenting them clearly and methodically. I have no doubt that this composition will serve as a most useful and valuable reference volume to the public.

I, therefore, extend my wishes and blessings to the esteemed author. May he continue dwelling in the tent of Torah and merit publishing many more scholarly volumes which expound upon other Torah disciplines.

CONGREGATION
Keter Torah

כ"ד סיון תשס"ז
12/06/07

לכל מאן דבעי,

ניתנה לי האפשרות לעיין ב"סדרי עריפות כצדקה", אני מכיר את מחבר הרי־שיכיה ומוצא את הספר בעל תובנה רבה
ועם נסיונות ברורים בהכברת חשיבות ההלכה בזמנים כדרנים אלו.

אני סמוך ובטוח כי ספר זה יחזק מצווה במיסיון זו.

בכבוד רב.

הרב שלום באוב

To the Honorable and Distinguished Rabbi Moshe Goldberger, Shlit"a,

It gave me great pleasure to see your wonderful words on the topic of the mitzvah

of *Tzedakah/Charity, Within Halacha And Agadah* . Your explanations are captivating

and eye opening and lead one towards the proper perspective , the Torah's perspective,

concerning the laws of *Tzedakah/Charity*.

May it be the will of the Al-mighty that your well spring of knowledge should

spread forth and awaken many to fulfill this most important Mitzvah which He

guarantees "tithe so that you will become rich, tithe so that you shall lack nothing." In

the *zichut* of this awakening , may we merit the end of our long exile as it says, "with

you (Avraham) do we sign/end " which our rabbis explain to mean, with the character

trait of kindness which you (Avraham) personify, may our exile be signed/ended.

B. Eisenberger

The National Synagogue ™

Ohev Sholom Talmud Torah Congregation

1600 Jonquil Street, NW, Washington, DC 20012-1199
Office 202.882.7225 Fax 202.882.0804 · TheNationalSynagogue.org
Rabbi Shmuel Herzfeld · Dr. Harold Brodsky, President

'I have read with great enjoyment Rav Goldberger's work about the priorities of Tzedakah.

This is a work that fills a great need. It will be of much interest and of enormous benefit to the Jewish community of America. It is a book that I enthusiastically recommend.

The American Jewish community is perhaps the wealthiest Jewish community in history. For this reason especially we need direct and unbiased guidance on how best to fulfill the mitzvah of Tzedakah. This book is a tremendous help in that respect.

Rav Goldberger's book is clearly written and easy to understand. It also contains great wisdom and an intricate knowledge of the sources.

I thank the author for sharing his deep knowledge on the topic with our community.

Sincerely,

Shmuel Herzfeld
Rabbi
Ohev Sholom—The National Synagogue®

Young Israel of Monsey & Wesley Hills
I. Edward Koppel Synagogue
בית ישראל איסר הלוי קאפפעל ז"ל

Rabbi Ari Jacobson
Morah D'asra

בס"ד עש"ק פ' וישלח תשס"ז לפ"ק

One can hardly imagine a *mitzvah* more important than that of *tzedaka;* the Talmud and Midrashim are filled with statements attributing our very existence to charitable giving.   Unfortunately, however, most of us are not yet blessed with unlimited resources, and we are therefore often faced with the need to prioritize our giving. Which causes take precedence? Is providing meals for hungry children overseas more important than supporting a local yeshiva in distress? Is the *halacha* different when the beneficiary is a relative?   What about your shul?   Can membership dues be applied towards *ma'aser kesafim*?

Priorities in Tzedaka addresses these issues and many others. The author, Rabbi Moshe Goldberger, is a well- known *talmid chacham* and *ba'al midos* who has previously graced the Jewish community with a host of informative and inspirational Torah works. We are confident that this current volume will be similarly well-received by scholar and layman alike, as it contains information of utmost importance to all.

With Blessings of Torah,

Rabbi Ari Jacobson

58 Parker Blvd. Monsey, New York 10952
(845) 362-1838

Rabbi Elie Karfunkel
446 Spadina Rd., Suite 206
Toronto, Ontario M5P 3M2
Fax: (416) 483-6712
rabbielie@foresthilljewishcentre.com

To Whom It May Concern:

Re: Letter of Approbation

The Torah tells us to be Holy. The will of Hashem isn't that we merely engage in acts of holiness, but more so that our core becomes Holy. Specifically, Tzedakah is not just about giving to others, but rather about transforming who we are by what we do.

This Sefer is an invaluable piece of work for two very important reasons. Firstly, it clarifies the difficult role in managing your Maaser Money. Secondly, and even more so, it makes you more mindful of what it is that you are doing and illustrates that by doing so, you are on the path of becoming Holy.

I know that many people will greatly benefit from your work. May you be blessed to continue strengthening our People.

Yasher Koach,

Rabbi Elie Karfunkel

A project of Ohr Somayach / Tanenbaum College International
Chicago • Cleveland • Detroit • Jerusalem • Johannesburg • London • Los Angeles • Miami • Montreal • New York • Odessa • Toronto

בס״ד

Eliyahu Kaufman
Rabbi
732-985-8360

Elizer Kaminetzky
Rabbi Emeritus
732- 249-1652

Stephen Stein
President
732-828-8764

Congregation
Ohav Emeth

415 Raritan Avenue
P.O. Box 1533
Highland Park
N.J. 08904

(732) 247-3038
Fax (732) 247-1483

November 6, 2006

To Whom It May Concern:

I am taking this opportunity to render my endorsement to the wonderful and precious book written by Rabbi Moshe Goldberger called Priorities of Tzedakah – may he live a good and long life. I have reviewed several chapters and I see that they are thoroughly wonderful and (the Torah concepts) explained lucidly.

Contained within this book are gems and pearls of sound reason and it is therefore desirable for every Torah person, Rabbi and teacher, to review (the material) in the book in order to inspire others.

May it be His Will that these gems be appreciated by all Torah people. How important it is for subject matter to be presented in a timely fashion.

With great respect and friendship,

Rabbi Eliyahu Kaufman

ראשית ירושלים

בס"ד י"ג תשרי תשס"ז

<u>מכתב ברכה</u>

לכבוד

ידידיי ר' משה ופריידה פייפער הי"ו

שלום רב,

שמחתי מאוד בראותי את הספר בהלכות צדקה שנטלתם חלק בהוצאתו.

"ביודענו ובמכירנו קאמינא", מכיר אני אתכם זה עשרות בשנים כעוסקים בצרכי ציבור באמונה חעושים כל ימיהם פעולות צדקה וחסד.

נפשכם הקשורה באומן מיוחד וציירתי בעבודת הצדקה העירה אתכם לשאלות רבות בענייני צדקר – שאלות שהופנו להרה"ג הרב גולדברג שליט"א הידוע בספריו תרבים בכל תחומי התורה וחיחדות מתלמידיו המובהקים של הגאון הרב ראובן פיינשטיין שליט"א. תשובותיו התקבצו לכדי הספר שלפנינו העוסק בשאלות החמורות של סדרי עדיפות בצדקה ועוד.

יה"ר שתזכו להמשיך עוד שנים רבות בחסד ובצדקה מתוך בריות גופא ונהורא מעליא. יתן ה' לכם נחת רבה מכל צאצאיכם ומתוך ברכה "והשיב לב אבות על בנים" תזכו לעלות לשכון קבע בארצינו הקדושה.

בעתירה ידידכם

[חתימה בכתב יד]

הרב יעקב צבי מרקוס

לפנים רב ק"ק ישראל הצעיר

סטאטן איילנד ניו יורק

כתובתנו: ת.ד 1390 גבעת שרת בית שמש 99523 ● טל' 9997155 – 02 ● פקס' 9997154 – 02

RABBI ARYEH RALBAG
1240 EAST 29 STREET
BROOKLYN, NEW YORK 11210
Phone: 718-258-5596 • Fax: 718-252-8418
Rav: Young Israel of Avenue K

אריה רלב"ג

רב ראשי ואב"ד דק"ק אשכנזים אמשטרדם, הולנד
יושב על מדין בבד"ץ אגודת הרבנים דאהב"ד וקנדה

ז' טבת תשס"ז

הנה כבוד ידידי הרב הגאון ר' משה גאלדבערגר שליט"א אשר יראתו קודמת לחכמתו ומרביץ תורה לרבים
ומורה בהרבה ענינים בשו"ת בהלכה,והביאו לפני קונטרסו החדש בעניני צדקה. והנה מביא מראשונים
ואחרונים ומוסיף נופת מדיליה , ואני מלא התפעלות מן בקיאותו בכל המסתעיף לענין זה, ובפרט מסברתו
הישרה והרחבה לאסוקי שמעתתא אליבא דהלכתא בשאלות צדקה אקטואלים השייכים לזמה"ז.
והנני מזרזו שיוציא לאור חדושים האלו שוודאי ראויים לדפוס שהם תועלת לרבים.
ולסיים הנני מברכו שיזכה להמשיך לגנת בתורה וירעלו ספריו על שלחן מלכים מאן מלכי רבנן
וע"ז באתי על החתום היום ז' טבת תשס"ז לפ"ק פק"ק ברוקלין
ממני המוקירו ביקרא דאורייתא

My Honored Friend, HaRav HaGaon Reb Moshe Goldberger, whose piety precedes his
wisdom and who spreads Torah to the masses and teaches Halacha in many practical
subjects. I read his manuscript "Priorities in Tzedaka" dealing with complicated issues in
charity / tzedaka. He quotes both sources in earlier and more recent Halachic works and
adds his own invaluable conclusions. I was impressed with his broad scope of Torah
knowledge in everything related to the subject matter at hand; especially his logical and
well reasoned conclusions to actual modern tzedaka problems. I urge him to publish
without delay his Halachic insights , which are both worthy to be published and will
greatly benefit the public.
In conclusion, I bless the author that he should merit to continue his holy task of delving
into the Torah and disseminating his works on the " Tables of Princes"; who are these
princes ? The Rabbinical Elite !
We hereby affix our signature 7 Teves 5767 in Brooklyn ,N.Y.
  By a good friend who honors him with the Honor of Torah

Congregation Adath Israel
of the
Jewish Educational Center

HaRav Pinchas M. Teitz z"tl
Founder

Rav Elazar M. Teitz
Mara D'Asra

Rabbi Jonathan Schwartz
Rav

Robert Moskowitz
Chairman of the Board

Board Members
Nancy Asher
Randi Bell
Secretary
Paul Gruber
Maddy Hoffman
Treasurer
Brian Hess
Treasurer
Dr. Yossi Pinsker
Vice-Chairman
Arthur Rosen
Friends Treasurer
Harry Stadler
Brenda Strashun
Rabbi Elchanan Weinbach

Advisory Committee
Marjorie Blenden

וזו השאלה שאל טורנוסרופוס הרשע את רבי עקיבא אם אלקיכם אוהב עניים הוא מפני מה
אינו מפרנסם? א"ל כדי שיניצל אנו בהם מדינה של גיהנם (בבא בתרא ט.)

"This question was posed by Turnus Rufus to Rabbi Akiva: 'If your God loves the
poor, why doesn't He support them?' Rabbi Akiva replied 'It is so, in order to afford
us the salvation from the punishment of Gehinnom.'" (Bava Basra 9a)

The Jewish life is one that is dedicated to Mitzva performance. Our Avos remind us of the need to perform as many Mitzvos in this world as possible. Chief among these Mitzvos is the Mitzva of Tzedaka (Rambam, Hil. Matnos Aniyim 10:1). For during the inception of Klal Yisroel, Avraham Aveinu was already told that the main purpose of our nation's existence was לעשות צדקה -- to perform acts of Tzedaka. In our Yamim Noraim liturgy, it is Tzedaka (together with Teshuva and Tefilla) that helps bring about the change of a bad decree. And our final redemption will be brought about through the great Mitzva of tzedaka as the Novi promises ושביה בצדקה -- the return to Zion will happen as a result of Tzedaka (Isaiah 1: 27).

But just how does one properly achieve all the great merits of the Mitzva of Tzedaka? Should we respond to the myriad of calls, mailings and other solicitations that we are bombarded with daily? In what order should we prioritize our Tzedaka appeals? How are we to guarantee that our limited Tzedaka funds are expended to afford the maximum benefit to our society and bring us closer to the final redemption? Rav Moshe Goldberger and Mr. Milton Pfeiffer have tackled these problems in a clear and concise manner helping each of us fully understand and structure our personal priorities in this great Mitzva. A venerable Rav and Posek, Rav Goldberger's insights are both practical and sagacious making this publication a valuable addition to every Torah home. Yashar Koach to the authors for a job well done!

ויהי"ר שבזכות כתיבת חוברת זו וקיומה נזכה לברכת הנביא "והיה מעשה הצדקה שלום"
(ישעיה לב:יז)

החותם למען תורה גולמדנה
והנני בן הרב הגאון
Rabbi Jonathan Schwartz
Rav

1391 North Avenue, Elizabeth, NJ 07208
(908) 354-7318

Beth David Synagogue
ק"ק בית דוד

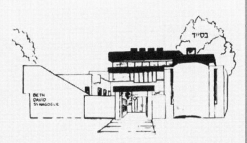

39 RIVERSIDE DRIVE   BINGHAMTON, N.Y. 13905
OFFICE (607) 722-1793
e-mail: bethdavid@stny.rr.com

ZEV SILBER, RABBI   AMINADAV ADAMIT, RABBI

RABBI'S STUDY / FAX (607) 722-7121

Saba, Wiesner,   President
Mark Budman, 1st Vice President
Aaron Alweis, 2nd Vice President

January 17, 2007
27 Tevet 5767

בס"ד

Dear Rabbi Goldberger,

I had the pleasurable opportunity of reviewing your *sefer* "Priorities in Tzedaka". The pamphlet deals primarily with *ma'aser kesafim* – the custom of designating 10% of our earnings and income to charitable causes. According to most opinions *ma'aser kesafim* is neither a Biblical or Rabbinic obligation, yet it is certainly a praiseworthy custom that has roots in Jewish life from time immemorial. This custom has been practiced in all Jewish communities at all times.

As with all *mitzvot*, we want to make sure that we observe this *mitzvah* in the proper way, following the dictates of the Code of Jewish Law and the concepts developed by our rabbis. This *sefer* is organized in a very logical way and written in easily understood language. This enables the student and reader to fully understand the concept of *tzedaka* and how to organize one's own charitable giving program. Every household would benefit by having this *sefer* available and accessible when making gifting decisions.

I found that the frequently repeated emphasis on the positive attitude that one should have when sharing his or her resources with others who are less fortunate, to be one of the most valuable lessons that are taught. Even though one fulfills the *mitzvah* by giving, one's attitude and positive demeanor reflect a person's understanding that G-d is the source of all the good that one possesses. This concept is underscored by the repeated emphasis that giving isn't only accomplished with money, but also includes giving of one's time and heartfelt caring.

I highly recommend this *sefer* to all who wish to better understand this wonderful *mitzvah*.

Sincerely yours,

Zev Silber
Rabbi

BINGHAMTON'S TRADITIONAL SYNAGOGUE
Affiliated with the Union of Orthodox Jewish Congregations of America

B''H

Young Israel of Queens Valley

141-55 77TH AVENUE. FLUSHING. NEW YORK 11367

(718) 263-3921. 263-9073 · FAX

PERETZ STEINBERG

RABBI

בס"ד י' אדר תשס"ז

הנה כבוד ידידי הרה"ג ר' משה גאלדבערגער שליט"א בא ותלמודו בידו היינו

החיבור שחיבר על עניני צדקה בכלל ועדיפיות בצדקה בפרט. והנה המחבר

שליט"א ירד בעומקן של הדברים ללבן העניינים באופן שנראה שיש סדר לצדקה

וכל דבר נתברר בלשון צח ונקי ונכלל בזה הספר הרבה שאלות ששאלו מכבוד

המחבר שליט"א ונתלבן הדינים על ידו ועכשיו מסדר דינים אלו בתוך ספרו

להראות מעלות הצדקה ודיני קדימת נתינת הצדקה מי ומי זוכין לקבל ראשון

ושני וכדומה. וכל זה נכתב בסדר הגון ובאופן שיהא קל על המעיינים בספר זה.

לכן אמינא לפעלא טבא שייש' כחו וחילו לאורייתא להגות בתורה יומם ולילה

ולהוציא חידושיו לאור עולם ויזכה כבוד המחבר שליט"א לאסוקי שמעתתא

אליבא דהלכתא ללמוד וללמד מתוך שמחה והרחבת הדעת.

ואני מברך הרב המחבר שליט"א שיפוצו מעינותיו חוצה וישיעלה דבריו על

שלחן מלכים מאן מלכי רבנן מתוך בריות גופא ונהורא מעליא.

הכותב וחותם למען כבוד התורה ולומדי' ומלמדי'.

פרץ שטיינבערג

Young Israel of Plainview

132 SOUTHERN PARKWAY
PLAINVIEW, N.Y. 11803

(516) 433-4811   www.YIPlainview.com   Rabbi@YIPlainview.com

בס"ד

Elie Weissman, Rabbi   *Kenneth Malc, President*

Rosh Chodesh Tevet, 5767
December 22, 2006

Dear Reader,

Expansive, collective responsibility represents the hallmark of the broader Jewish community. Our commitment to ideals of loving-kindness, altruism, and philanthropy has carried us through generations of exile. Indeed, even amidst great suffering and affliction, Jews throughout history expressed deep commitment to the care and sustenance of their brothers and sisters. No doubt this passionate consistency emerged from the ethical inspiration of Halacha; the codification of the laws of *tzedakah va'chesed* exists as a Jew's constant reminder of his/her responsibility to the members of *Am Yisrael*.

Globalization and advanced communications have created numerous opportunities for philanthropy and assistance in America and in *Eretz Yisrael*. Wholly committed to an individual community while concurrently inundated daily with requests from sincere organizations positively affecting the Jewish world, the modern Jew is often left confused and overwhelmed. Rabbi Moshe Goldberger's <u>Priorities in Tzedaka: Higher forms of giving</u> offers concise and practical guidance in the "art" and Mitzvah of giving in the modern world. Further, Rabbi Goldberger's sources and direction can inspire further study and research in the topics of *tzedaka*.

Ultimately, giving, whether more or less, flows directly out of a Jewish heart. <u>Priorities in Tzedaka</u> can help positively channel that desire and commitment. I encourage you to take the time to read this book and utilize it in setting your own philanthropic priorities.

Sincerely,

Rabbi Elie Weissman

Introduction

This book, *B'ezras Hashem*, attempts to clarify our *halachic* obligation to give *tzedaka* by outlining the sources from *Tanach, Talmud,* the *Rishonim,* and the *Acharonim.* After having established why it is important to give *tzedaka,* this book elaborates on what our *tzedaka* priorities are, on how to give, and on how to become more giving. The book outlines the benefits that come from giving *tzedaka,* and concludes with a game plan for how to approach giving *tzedaka* so that it becomes an integral part of daily life.

■ CAUTION

We caution our readers not to change their giving style dramatically before reading through and studying this entire work, and discussing their ideas and conclusions with their own competent *halachic* advisor.

■ MAKING PLANS

There are five suggestions to keep in mind when we make plans about giving charity:

1. Decide that your ideas and thoughts should not be considered as a definite pledge until you actually get the funds to their destination.

2. Use a *Bli Neder* system (decide that you do not want to be obligated by any type of vows) to avoid complications associated with vows.

3. Leave yourself options to make adjustments as you learn the laws, etc.

4. Leave yourself flexibility for errors or miscalculations.
5. You may opt for specific applications of your choice, in some cases.

■ YOUR PLAN

The road to proper giving is a bit complicated and requires analysis to develop a thoughtful and effective program for each person. You have to consider who you are – what are your motives and your means. You have to think about what kinds of causes you want to give more to and why. You need to learn how to evaluate the issues and organizations and how to gauge your levels of giving.

Buying a house, for example, is a personal and emotional decision, but you also need a competent engineer's report to make a wise decision. You need to study basic information about the community, about real estate values and about the local *shuls* and *yeshivos*. Similarly, when it comes to the great *mitzvah* issue of giving charity, there are many aspects we need to clarify in order to maximize our giving opportunities.

We are going to analyze the 22 questions asked on pages 31 and 32 in the book as general guideposts. (Corresponding to the twenty-two letters of the Hebrew *Aleph-Beis*, the building blocks that *Hashem* used to design the Torah and the world.) We will also be dealing with numerous related issues as well.

FOREWORD

I was brought up in a household that was imbued with love of *tzedaka* and *gemilas chesed*. When I married, I joined a wonderful family with similar notions of love and commitment to *Klal Yisroel*. As my own family grew, and my interaction with numerous other like-minded community activists expanded, it became evident that we all had numerous *halachic* questions on *tzedaka* priorities, questions which left our contributions subject to our individual uncertainty.

This wonderful book, *Priorities in Tzedaka: Higher Forms of Giving*, is the best *sefer* yet written to help every Jew prioritize *tzedaka* giving in a *halachically* appropriate manner, and I am extremely grateful for the opportunity to be one of the sponsors of its publication.

The undertaking of this project by Nachas Unlimited is a wonderful gift, given to the entire Jewish community. Nachas Unlimited is an organization whose role in assisting sick and injured Jewish children throughout the world is universally known. It was established by Milton Pfeiffer, whose life's blood is *tzedaka* and beneficial community activism. I have enjoyed a four-decade-long relationship with Milton, and I look forward to at least four more decades of the same.

The initiation of this project by Milton began with his letter of inquiry to numerous *Rabbanim*, seeking their guidance for the distribution of his annual *tzedaka* in a *halachically* correct manner. We are all the recipients of numerous requests for *tzedaka* from many worthy institutions in our community, in neighboring communities, from throughout North America and from

Israel and throughout the world. It is almost impossible to give a meaningful contribution to all of the *tzedakos*, and therefore *halachic* guidance in prioritization is essential. Milton sought written guidance so that he and others could follow the suggestions thereafter.

It was for this reason that Milton Pfeiffer approached Rabbi Moshe Goldberger, a well-known scholar, to do in-depth research, and then to write a detailed response to Milton's *tzedaka* inquiry. As the response grew in size and substance, the project developed into this *sefer*. It is well written, organized and encompassing, and it should serve as a useful guide for all of us in the giving of our *tzedaka* in the proper *halachic* fashion.

Prior to its publication, the draft of the book was sent to more than a dozen *Rabbanim* for their *haskomos,* and who added their input where appropriate. The *Haskomos* come from renowned *Rabbanim* from around the world, and they should add to your confidence in utilizing this *sefer*. Of course, every individual should consult his own *Rav* for final decisions.

As part of Nachas Unlimited's communal *tzedaka* efforts, it is distributing free copies of this work to synagogues and *yeshiva* high schools throughout the United States as a reference book for consultation on the issues of *tzedaka* priorities. I also encourage all readers to contribute to Nachas Unlimited to assist it in numerous worthy *tzedaka* activities.

With wishes for health, happiness and success to all of the readers of this *sefer* and to *Klal Yisrael* through the coming of *Mashiach*, I remain,

Saul E. Feder, Esq.

PREFACE

An Open Letter About Tzedaka

Dear Rabbi:

We live, B"H, in a wonderful community in New York. We were always taught that giving *tzedaka* is a most important *mitzvah* of *Hashem*'s Torah, and therefore we see this as a priority in our lives. However, we are sometimes overwhelmed by numerous requests for charity donations.

These requests come as we walk down the street near our local grocery store, at weddings, and at *shul*. There are knocks on our door and phone solicitations from worthy causes, hurricane funds, and from relief organizations. There are requests in the mail signed by reputable *Rabbanim*.

Of course, there are also causes that are close to our hearts, such as the schools our children attended, the schools we attended, and the causes of the Rabbi who has been our spiritual mentor for the past thirty years.

There are also community organizations such as our *shul*, the *mikveh*, and other schools in the community that our children did not attend. In addition, there are lifesaving organizations such as Hatzoloh, Tomchei Shabbos, keren *yesomim* (orphans), and *hachnasas kallah* (for needy brides), both locally and in Eretz Yisroel.

How much *tzedaka* are we obligated to give?

To whom are we required to give, and how much should we give to each person or each cause?

Is our children's school tuition considered *tzedaka*?

Is *shul* membership considered *tzedaka*?

If our grown children ask for money to help them with their children's tuition, is that considered *tzedaka*?

What if our children live in *Eretz Yisroel*; does this impact on how important it is for us to give to their causes?

What if my children from *Eretz Yisroel*, who learn and teach Torah, want to come visit us here? Can buying them a ticket be considered *tzedaka*?

How much money should we put aside for a *yahrzeit* or at *Yizkor* for our parents to support a cause that was close to their hearts?

How much should be set aside for *kaporos, matonos le'evyonim, and maos chitin,* and are these *mitzvos* separate from the *mitzvah* of *tzedaka*?

Is lending someone money considered *tzedaka*?

Is buying an ad to honor a friend or buying a raffle ticket for worthy institutions *tzedaka*?

What about a concert or production where the proceeds are used to benefit poor people?

Does the mitzvah of *tzedaka* apply specifically to giving money, or should we also volunteer our time and energy as well?

How important is it to support Torah study?

How do I balance my own desire to retire and study Torah with the implication that I will no longer have as much money to distribute to *tzedaka*?

We earn about $100,000 net after taxes, from which we are trying to allocate charity for the various causes, in order of importance and dollar amounts. Please help clarify these matters for us and for others who have these questions as well.

Mr. & Mrs. Concerned Couple

Author's Note

The questions in the letter have been divided into twenty-two categories, listed below. Answers may be found on the pages given.

THE OBLIGATION TO GIVE TZEDAKA

Torah sources for giving
Why do we have this mitzvah?
Who are we required to give to?
How much is too much?

TORAH SOURCES FOR GIVING

- עשר תעשר – Give a tenth, Give a tenth (*Dvarim*, 14:22)
- פתוח תפתח – Open, open (your hand) (*ibid*, 15:8)
- נתון תתן – Give, give (*ibid*, 15:10)
- פתוח תפתח – Open, open (ibid, 15:11)

This amazing sequence of double expressions, four times, in *Hashem's* Torah, opens our eyes to the unique *mitzvah* of opening up our hearts, minds, and hands to giving generously.

Furthermore, we are commanded: "Do not harden your heart nor close your hand" (*Devarim*, 15:7). This is explained as meaning that we are required to give to anyone in need who asks, not to turn away a person empty handed, and to even give to those who are reluctant to ask but are truly in need.

■ TEN PERCENT

How much of our income should be designated to *tzedaka*?

The general guideline is to contribute at least 10% of our income for *tzedaka*. This is derived from several sources in *Tanach* when our *Avos* (forefathers) gave *maaser'*-a tenth – of their possessions. Avraham Avinu, (*Breishis*, 14:20), gave Malkitzedek *maaser* from everything that he gained at that time. Yaakov Avinu (*Breishis*, 28:22), made a vow that if he came back safe from the ordeal with Lavan, "Of all that You shall give me, I shall give You a tenth." They recognized that God is the One Who provides us with everything, and as such, by giving to those who serve God, and to those designated by God, we are showing our gratitude to *Hashem.*

[The Rambam, (*Melochim*, 9:1) actually says that Yitzchok was the first to separate *maaser.* The Raavad, however, objects and says it was Avraham who gave first (see *Kesef Mishna).*]

■ A Fifth

"עשר אעשרנו לך" (*Breishis*, 28:22).

When we look closer at this source it actually says, "I will give a tenth and a tenth," which is two tenths – which equals a fifth. The *Shulchan Aruch Yoreh Deah* (*Siman* 249) says the ideal is to give a fifth. The Prisha explains that this is derived from Yaakov Avinu, who gave a fifth. Thus, we learn the ideal is to give a fifth, but for average people, a tenth is sufficient.

■ From all profits

This idea is also taught in regard to our obligation to support *Kohanim* and *Leviim.* They were devoted to serve *Hashem,* and therefore we are required to "Give *maaser* from **all** of the produce that comes forth from your field each year," (*Devarim,* 14:22). *Tosfos* (*Taanis,* 9a) explains that the word "all" teaches us to give a tenth from all of our net earnings, including merchandise, profitable stock market transactions, interest and dividends, etc. Similarly, in certain years of the *Shemita* cycle we were obligated to give *maaser* to various groups of people. Nowadays, most of us do not have farms that produce crops. Thus, it is incumbent upon us to put aside money from the income that *Hashem* blesses us with, and to use that money to support the poor and those that serve God.

■ WHY TEN?

What is the significance of ten? Why is *maaser* a tenth and not 6%, 7% or 12%? A unique symbolism can be discerned in the principle of this *mitzvah*. *Maaser* of a flock is a tenth of "all that pass under the rod" (*Vayikra*, 27:32) of the shepherd. *Hashem*, the great shepherd of our nation (*Tehilim*, 80:2), observed the generations pass before Him until He saw the excellence of the "tenth" (Avraham Avinu) and He declared: "The tenth shall be holy to *Hashem*" (*Vayikra*, 27:32). "There were ten generations from Noach until Avraham Avinu, who came and merited the reward of all of them" (*Avos*, 5:2). Therefore, Avraham's chosen descendents are holy to *Hashem* (*Yirmiya*, 2:3). Thus we demonstrate our gratitude to God for choosing us to be His chosen "tenth" by dedicating a tenth to His service (Rav A. Miller, *ztl*). [Avraham was also the twentieth from Adam which alludes to a "fifth."]

Avraham (*Breishis*, 13), Yitzchok (*Breshis*, 26), and Yaakov, were all very wealthy and they gave *tzedaka*, *maaser* and *chomesh* generously. We, as their descendants, should strive to emulate their ways in everything we do.

STEP TWO

WHY DO WE HAVE THIS MITZVAH?

First of all, we give *tzedaka* because *Hashem* commanded us to – we do not need more of a reason. However, there are some obvious benefits and results of this *mitzvah*. When we give *tzedaka* we are honoring God our Creator and Provider and displaying our gratitude to Him for all that He has given us. This giving, in turn, brings us closer to *Hashem*.

When we give to those who are needy who serve God, we demonstrate that we view our possessions as a gift from God and not as belonging to us. Giving is a tangible way to practice developing our trust in *Hashem*, since *Hashem* promises: "Give a tenth to others in need, so that you will become wealthy" (*Taanis,* 9a). What is wealth for? Why should we desire wealth? Just to keep money in the bank or to waste it? Shouldn't we give for the sake of the *mitzvah*? *Rabeinu* Chananel explains that one should desire to do the *mitzvah* of giving continuously. But how can we keep on giving? Aren't we going to run out of funds?

The answer is, "Give *maaser* so that *Hashem* will bless you with more and more, and you will be able to keep on giving more!"

You also change and improve as you give, thus you become a more deserving person.

Pirkei Avos (3:7) teaches:

תֶּן לוֹ מִשֶּׁלּוֹ – Give Him from His

שָׁאַתָּה וְשֶׁלְּךָ שֶׁלּוֹ – for you and yours are His!

■ OBSERVE THE PROCESS

We can ask, "Why does *Hashem* ask us to please test Him by giving *maaser,* " (*Malachi,* 3:10)? Indeed, this is the only *mitzvah* where we are encouraged to "test" *Hashem.*

The Malbim explains that it does not say the word *Nisoyon,* which would mean to see if *Hashem* will come through for us. We are certain that He can do as He pleases and that He will never fail us, as long as it is for our benefit. We also pray daily in the morning blessings "that *Hashem* should not test us." Thus we should strive to avoid being "tested."

Instead, the word used in *Malachi* is from the root of the word *bechina,* which means an examination, a keeping of records to see how *Hashem* will cause us to prosper. Thus, giving *tzedaka* is an opportunity to witness the resulting rewards and to see how *Hashem* runs the world.

Why does this apply only to the *mitzvah* of *tzedaka* and not in regard to other *mitzvos,* such as keeping *Shabbos,* eating kosher, etc.? The reason may be that it could be difficult to give away money that you toiled long and hard for, without receiving any tangible benefit. With other *mitzvos,* it is straightforward to see how you derive personal benefit, although it may cost you money. When giving *tzedaka* though, a person may feel that there is nothing in it for him. *Hashem* responds by assuring us that by giving *tzedaka* we will gain tremendous prosperity.

There is an additional insight which the Satmar Rebbe, *ztl,* offers. When we hire workers to harvest our crops, we are required to let them eat of the fruits while at work, but only if they are actually harvesting the fruit, not if they are only repairing the fences. Similarly, *Hashem* says, in general, with all other *mitzvos,*

"I will provide eternal rewards in abundance and some fringe benefits in this world. However, for this *mitzvah*, since you are providing funds for others, you will also get to enjoy an increase of those funds, measure for measure, as you keep giving to others."

■ GIVING EQUALS GAINING

Some add that of course *Hashem* rewards us for all *mitzvos* that we perform. It may be difficult to comprehend that giving will result in gaining money. Thus *Hashem* encourages us to try it out and see the incredible results (*Kochav M'Yaakov*).

In addition, God rewards us not only for doing His *mitzvos*, but also for how we perform them with joy and enthusiasm. Thus, we are informed about some of the fringe benefits so that we should increase our joy in performing this great deed (*Arvei Nachal*).

■ DOUBLE MITZVAH

The Talmud (*Baba Basra*, 10a) states that it is obvious that *Hashem* loves the poor since He instructs us to care for them. But then why doesn't *Hashem* provide for the poor directly? The solution to this seeming contradiction is that He also loves the rich, and thus He instructs and allows them to help the poor so that they should merit rewards for doing this *mitzvah*. Hence, giving *tzedaka* is a double *mitzvah*: it helps the needy and enables *Hashem* to justify showering us with blessings as we become more worthy.

■ EXCEPTION

What about a seeming exception – a person who gives a tenth, but does not seem to be prospering? There are two possible explanations: He may have some other failings for which he deserves poverty. Thus his *maaser* giving may save him from a greater loss. Alternatively, he may be receiving wealth in other forms such as atonement for his sins, etc. (*Derech Sicha*, p. 562).

■ 24 / 7

The *mitzvah* of *tzedaka* is all pervasive and is always timely. It can be performed any time of day or night, each and every day of the year, by men and women alike. No one ever knows when a request for funds will be made. The giving never ceases. From the time we get our first dollar until the day we leave this earth, we must continue to give.

Of course we do not handle money on *Shabbos* or *Yom Tov,* but even then the *Shulchan Aruch,* (303:6) says: We do make pledges for charity for the poor or for the needs of a *shul.*

STEP THREE

WHO ARE WE REQUIRED TO GIVE TO?

■ ONESELF

You are your closest relative. As the Ramoh says, "One's own needs come before all others" (*Ramoh, Yoreh Deah*, 251:3). One is not obligated to give *maaser* if one is unable to support his own basic needs and that of his wife and children living at home. (*Aruch HaShulchan, Yoreh Deah*, 251:5). However, the *Mishna Brura* (156:2) cautions a person not to be deceived by the Evil Inclination who may claim that he always "needs" more and more for himself. A person should think: "What is necessary for me, without which I could not exist?" Furthermore, the Chofetz Chaim, in a footnote, urges us to consider as necessary for ourselves only that which we would provide to support someone else if we were obligated to do so.

What if a person were in a situation where he had only one container of water? If he should keep it for himself he would live, but someone else might die. If he would share the water, both of them might die.

The *Talmud* (*Bava Metzia*, 62a) gives two opinions on this situation:

1. Share the water
2. Keep the water for yourself

The *halacha* follows the second opinion. You are obligated to love others as you love yourself, but your own life must come first.

What about giving all the water to another person? That is forbidden because you have a Torah obligation to care for yourself first. Since you own the container of water, and since *Hashem* provided it for you to utilize, you must use it to save yourself.

Of course, in saving yourself you will also do your best to find more water with which to save others as well.

Thus we learn that *Hashem* will help us when we keep on the right path and when we keep our priorities straight.

■ OTHERS

After caring for yourself, your spouse, and your dependent children, you should not turn down legitimate requests from worthwhile people or causes. Thus the Tur, (*Shulchan Aruch, Yoreh Deah* 251), begins with

"כל הפושט ידיו ליטול, נותנין לו, אפי' נכרי"

"Anyone who stretches out his hand for charity, we should give them (at least a small amount) including even a non-Jew."

■ REQUESTS BY MAIL

An exception to this rule is that one is not obligated to send money to every letter request, only to a direct personal request.

One suggestion that applies to mailings is to take a moment to say a prayer for all the needy people we read about. This is a great *mitzvah*, for even when we may be short on funds, we have great powers at our disposal to say a prayer, such as, "*Hashem*, Master of the Universe, please help these individuals."

As regards mailings, according to *halacha* and according to government laws, one is not required to send anything back, when you did not request the mailing, even when an organization sends you a gift. It is yours to keep if you like, to give away to others, or to write "return to sender" on the package and send it back without costing you anything.

However, to just throw away all of the envelopes one receives goes against the principle of *rachmanus* (the Jewish trait of compassion) (*Rav Y. Belsky, shlita*).

If you have the desire to send money to each one, or have enough money to hire someone to respond with even a small sum to each and every envelope, it is praiseworthy. There is an anonymous donor who sends back a dollar to each cause with the following inspiring note:

> *"Dear Distinguished Servant of Hashem,*
>
> *Please accept this small donation with a big prayer request from us to Hashem that your assets should multiply with Hashem's blessings, and if healing is needed, may it come swiftly and completely.*
>
> *I regret that I am unable to contribute more at the present time, but I thank you wholeheartedly for allowing me to participate in this great mitzvah in a small measure. I hope to be able to do more in the future.*
>
> *May the redemption come swiftly in the merits of your worthwhile cause."*

If this is not a doable option, you should select some of the causes to respond to with the guidelines we will explain later on.

■ GRATITUDE

When you do receive a gift in the mail that you decide to use and benefit from, it is recommended to send a donation to the senders in gratitude; also consider the nature of the cause, its relevance to you and its merits.

■ At the Door

Rav Chaim Kanievsky, *Shlita,* was asked: if someone rings your doorbell for *tzedaka,* are you required to answer the door? He answered that it is better to answer and then apologize if you are unable to give. But if the person may think that you are not home, there is no prohibition if you do not go to the door (*Nezer HaChaim* p. 68).

■ A Problem / A Practical Solution

How should one deal with a collector who comes to the door and, when you offer him two dollars, he says, "It's not enough. I need to talk to you"?

First, you listen to his story. But what if you realize that you still can only give him a few dollars now?

The solution is to prepare a few sealed, dark-colored envelopes with a few dollars in them. You listen to the collector's story, and then you present him with an envelope and wish him *hatzlacha.*

■ Caution

Another exception is to avoid helping wicked people or wicked causes (see *Yoreh Deah* 251:1-2). The Torah does not say, "Give money to all poor people." Rather, the Torah instructs us to give *"tzedaka"* – which means "righteous charity giving." Thus, if a drug addict asks for money, we should be careful not to give him cash, which would be enabling him in his wickedness. We may help him get drug rehabilitation instead.

■ ALWAYS GIVE

We learn, "Do not turn away a suffering person in shame" (*Tehilim,* 74:21). One should always give at least a small amount (*Yoreh Deah,* 249:4). How much is considered a small amount? The *halachic* source says, "Give even a fruit." We can explain that the key is not to "shame" the person (ibid). Thus, a dollar may suffice, or even fifty cents or a quarter, depending on the person's stature and needs and on your assets, but the example is to give at least the value of a small fruit which could serve as a snack.

■ HIGHEST CHARITY

Several types of giving are listed as the highest form of giving *tzedaka*:

1. Redeeming captives (*Rambam, Laws of Charity,* 8:10): "There is no greater *mitzvah* than this." This refers to cases where lives are in danger.

2. Helping people get married (*Shulchan Aruch,* Yoreh Deah, 249:15): "There is no *tzedaka* greater than this." This applies even to people who are able to cover their budget ordinarily, but who are unable to cover the expenses that are essential to marry off their children (*Derech Sicha,* p. 552).

3. Some say supporting a *shul* is greater than helping a couple get married (*Shulchan Aruch,* 249:16). *Rav* Avigdor Miller, *ztl,* explained why this is such a great priority. A *shul* is supposed to be the central organization in a community, where Jews gather to pray to Hashem for all of their needs, to study Torah, and to focus on helping each other in every way. Thus it is an all-encompassing *mitzvah* to support a *shul*.

4. Supporting people studying Torah (*Shulchan Aruch,* 249:16): some say this is even greater than supporting a *shul*.

5. Helping a sick person (*Shulchan Aruch,* 249:16): some say this is also greater that supporting a *shul.*
6. Enabling someone to get a job (*Rambam,* 10:7): "There is no greater level of *tzedaka.*"

The Rambam summarizes the great concept of these *mitzvos*: "אין שמחה גדולה וגדולה ומפוארה" – "Helping the poor, orphans, widows, and converts – There is no greater and more glorious form of joy than making these people happy, for this is how we emulate *Hashem!*" (*Rambam, Laws of Megilah,* 2:17)

■ SIX TYPES

Thus, we have the six highest levels of priority in giving *tzedaka*: saving a life, enabling marriage, supporting a *shul,* spiritual welfare, health and providing an income. Which of these is actually the highest form of them all? The answer is that there are three stages of life needs: emergency life saving, personal and family fulfillment, and financial needs. Helping an individual with their specific needs at the present time is the greatest form of *tzedaka* for that person. Thus, if someone is in captivity and his life is in danger, to save him is the greatest *mitzvah.* Once he has been saved, marriage may be his greatest need. If he needs an income, then that would be most essential. Everyone also needs to study Torah regularly, for that is our true, highest purpose in life.

■ SUPER-GREAT

Regarding redeeming captives, which is a tremendous *mitzvah* (*Shulchan Aruch,* Yoreh Deah, 252:1), Rambam (8:10) calls this a *mitzvah gedola* (great) and *raboh* (super) *mitzvah.* The reason this is such a great *mitzvah* is because it is saving captives' lives. If their lives are out of danger now, the *mitzvah* is a lesser priority.

The Chofetz Chaim (*Ahavas Chesed,* 2:20:2) differentiates between actual life-saving, which is a greater priority, and redeeming captives from a situation that is not life-threatening.

To sum up: the six highest *tzedaka* priorities are:
• Rescuing someone when their life is in danger
• Helping someone get married
• Supporting a *shul*
• Helping promote Torah study
• Providing assistance with health
• Getting someone a job

But of these, which is the top of the line? *Rav* Chaim Kanievsky, *Shlita,* says it depends on which is most urgent now (*Nezer Ha-Chaim,* p. 60).

But what if they are all about the same level of urgency?

In *Derech Sicha* (p. 561) we learn that if there is no actual current emergency we go back to the general rule that, "Torah study is the greatest of all *mitzvos*" (*Peiah* 1:1). Thus, to support Torah education would be priority number one.

■ FIVE FINGERS

The Gr"a asks: why does the Torah use the expression, "Do not close your hand" regarding *tzedaka*? He answers that when your hand is closed, all the fingers seem to be the same size. However, when you open your hand, you see that each finger is a different size. So too, with *tzedaka*, each situation is unique. At times a *mitzvah* to marry off a couple in dire need is so urgent that it supersedes the support of Torah study, but at other times, Torah support is the greater priority (*Teshuvos V'Hanhagos*, vol. 1. p. 380).

We can ask:

How do these six cases fit in to the three word summary of this topic in *Mishlei* (Chap. 10) – "צדקה תציל ממות" – "Charity saves from death?"

The answer may be derived from the Talmud, which defines four types of death: "Four are considered as dead: the pauper, the leper, the blind and the childless" (*Nedorim*, 64b).

Tosfos explains that as we pray for life, we should also pray to be spared from these four types of afflictions.

We can now explain the six types of death that *tzedaka* saves us from:

Physical death-health and safety

Spiritual death-*shul* and *yeshiva*

Financial death-jobs

Social and Emotional death – marriage

■ A Story of Gains & Losses

The Talmud (*Baba Basra*, 10a) teaches that just as a person's sustenance is designated by *Hashem* at *Rosh Hashana*, so, too, his losses are prearranged. One who merits can give it as charity. One who does not merit, it may be confiscated by the government.

There is a story that tells of the nephews of Rabbi Yochanon ben Zakai. He had a dream that they were going to lose 700 silver coins that year. He therefore kept on coming to them to collect from them for *tzedaka* causes. Over the year he collected 683 coins from them. Before the end of the year the government had them brought in on some charges. Rabbi Yochanon told them, "Do not worry. It will not cost you more than seventeen coins," and he revealed the dream. They asked: "Why didn't you tell us outright?" He said, "This way, you fulfilled the mitzvah "לשמה" – for its own sake."

■ THE CONCEPT

This story is based on the concept taught in *Avos* (3:5). "One who accepts upon himself the yoke of Torah will be relieved from the yoke of the government and from that of *"Derech Eretz"* (the toil of earning a livelihood)."

Thus, by giving *tzedaka* adequately, a person can earn an exemption from having to suffer other forms of losses.

STEP FOUR

How much is too much?

The rule of giving a tenth of one's net earnings is considered the average measure of giving. The ideal measure for a generous person is to give a fifth, as is clearly stated in *Shulchan Aruch* (*Yoreh Deah,* 239:1). The Talmud (*Kesubos, Daf* 50) cautions that one who desires to be generous should not give more than a fifth, for he may then become impoverished and need to accept charity himself.

■ DIVIDE IT

When giving a fifth, it is also advisable to separate the amount into two "tenths," one of which should be given primarily to support those who study Torah and the other for other *mitzvah* causes (*Ahavas Chesed,* 2:19). This is why the Torah uses the expression, "I will give a tenth and a tenth."

■ SEVEN EXCEPTIONS

The Chofetz Chaim (*Ahavas Chesed,* 2:20) states that there are seven cases when one may, or at times is even obligated to, give even more than a fifth, either relating to special needs (1, 2 and 5) or relating to the type of giver (3, 4 and 7).

1. To save a life (or redeem a captive).
2. If the needy person is in front of you.
3. If the giver is a wealthy person who will probably not become needy, even if he gives more than a fifth.
4. If the giver has an ongoing steady income with which to support himself.

5. For the support of Torah study one is permitted to give more, because one acquires eternal shares of the Torah study he supports. The more one gives, the more shares one acquires. One becomes a partner with the Torah scholar as Yisocher and Zevulun formed a partnership. The Chofetz Chaim does not say how much the supporters gave or can give, but he does say they gave "much more than a fifth!" He then adds: "The more you give, the more shares you gain of the Torah you are supporting."

6. One who spends money on frivolous indulgences cannot justify not spending more when it comes to *mitzvah* objectives.

7. One who is close to death may also give away more of his assets. Some say as much as he desires, and some say only up to a third of his assets, or up to half.

Note: some add also that as a merit to achieve atonement for sins, one may give more than a fifth to charity (*Derech Emunah*, 7:26:51).

■ OTHER FORMS OF GIVING

Do not think that you should stop being a giving person when you are short on funds. We are obligated to be givers all the time, in all of our transactions with everyone we interact with. We need to share with people kind words, encouragement, hope, and caring, and to provide them with a sense of importance. You can always reach out and help others become their best. You can always make a difference by helping others with your smile and caring attitude.

With the right attitude and sensitivity to other people's needs, you can make them feel special when they sense your sincere caring heart, kind words, helping hands, and also your financial assistance.

The Vilna Gaon says: "If you give a coin to a poor person who is starving and you save his life, you gain a much greater *mitzvah* than if he was not about to die. It is as if you saved a whole world and you gain a tremendous merit" (Commentary to *Russ,* 2:19).

If there is a choice between providing for the needs of a woman over taking care of a man, it is preferable to provide for the woman. A man can beg from door to door, whereas a woman would be embarrassed and find this demeaning.

■ STORY OF A WEDDING GIFT

Rabbi Akiva once met stargazers who told him that his daughter would die of a snake bite on the day of her wedding. He was concerned, and we can be sure that he prayed for her safety.

On her wedding day she happened to stick a pin into the wall, which landed in the eye of a snake, thus saving her life.

In the morning she saw the dead snake and spoke to her father. He asked her what *mitzvah* she had performed the day before. She told him that there was a poor person at the door, but everyone was busy preparing for the wedding feast, so no one heard him. She took her portion and gave it to him. Her father said: "That *mitzvah* of charity saved you from death" (*Shabbos,* 156b).

- What is the significance that the snake was killed in its eye?
- Why did this episode occur on her wedding day?

We can explain that the goal of marriage is for each spouse to learn to see the needs of the other. This was the test she passed when she saw the needs of a poor person on that special day. Thus *Hashem* arranged for her to kill the snake in its eye!

■ To Win

All you need is the desire and dream to give and help others, and a dollar to share...

SECTION 2

AN INDIVIDUAL'S
TZEDAKA PRIORITIES

Who is responsible to give?

Who comes first in our responsibility to give?

Why are these the Priorities?

Supporting Torah Study

STEP FIVE

WHO IS RESPONSIBLE TO GIVE?

Do men and women have the same obligation to give *tzedaka*? A woman is obligated to give *tzedaka* (*Sefer Hachinuch*, Mitzvah 479), and until she is married, she has the same guidelines as a man. A married woman takes into account her husband's input, and factors such as which spouse is earning the money, and whether anyone else is helping to support them (*Shulchan Aruch, Yoreh Deah*, 248:4 and *Pischei Teshuva*). A couple should discuss their plans with each other and also seek the advice of a competent Rav.

Do children have an obligation to give *tzedaka?*

- It is ideal to train children to give *maaser* from their spending money (allowance).
- If minors receive monetary gifts which they put into savings, they are obligated to give *maaser* on the money when they come of age- 12 for a girl and 13 for a boy (*Psak* from *Rav* S.Z. Auerbach, *ztl*).
- Teenagers who receive funds from their parents for specific needs are not required to give *maaser* on the monies received.

■ PAYING DEBTS

What if a person has outstanding debts? *Derech Emunah (Laws of Gifts to the Poor*, Chap 7:96) writes that he should not give much *tzedaka* until he pays off his debts. This means that he should not give more than a minimum of $10 a year to charity, and for his own needs he should be frugal until he finishes paying off his debts. But he also quotes the Chazon Ish who recommends that he keep a record of the *maaser* that he is not giving now, so that after paying off his bills he can pay this *maaser*.

פריעת בעל חוב – מצוה! Paying off one's debts is a *mitzvah* (*Kesubos*, 86a)! One who borrows but does not plan to pay off those debts is described as having the worst of all character flaws (*Avos*, 2:9), for he is demonstrating a lack of gratitude for the kindness he is receiving. It is considered a form of theft if he refuses to pay a debt when it is due. If he is unable to pay, he has to contact the lender to apologize for the delay (*Derech Sicha,* p. 303).

One who owes money for his children's tuition or who receives financial assistance to help pay his children's tuition bill should not be spending *maaser* money for other causes until he pays off his tuition bill priority. He may give small amounts to other causes, but his primary focus must be to pay off his debts first.

■ TUITION FIRST

One has to pay full tuition for his children's Yeshiva education before taking expensive vacations, decorating a home or buying items that are not considered as necessities but luxuries.

■ WHAT TO SAY

If a lender feels that he cannot lend money to a certain individual because he does not think

1. that the borrower will be able to repay him, or
2. he does not trust him,

what should he say to avoid insulting the person?

- Some say one can say, "I don't have funds available," i.e., meaning not for him. This is not considered an untruth in these circumstances (*Titen Emes L'Yaakov* 5:15).

• Others say one should avoid saying words that may transgress "אל תפתח פה לשטן" – "Don't open your mouth which might leave room for the Satan." Rather than say "I don't have," say "Let me look into it," or some other excuse.

■ PRIORITIES IN SPENDING

If a poor person receives funds earmarked for his family's household needs, he may not use them to pay off a debt (*Igros Moshe, Yoreh Deah*, 1:152). He may not even borrow from these funds to pay off his debt, because the person who gave the money earns a greater *mitzvah* of *tzedaka* by giving it for his basic home needs.

By opening up your home and your wallet to give more, you will gain more (*Derech Eretz Zuta*-9.)

STEP SIX

WHO COMES FIRST IN OUR RESPONSIBILITY TO GIVE?

As we mentioned in Step Three, you must first take care of your own basic needs and those of your immediate family. Your spouse is considered as an extension of yourself; thus, a husband and wife are considered as one person.

Even if you are unable to give to others, it is still recommended that you calculate and separate *maaser* and then use that money for your own needs (*Minchas Yitzchok,* 6:101).

It is also important to keep in mind that one is still required to try to give something to those in need who ask for help, and not to turn away a person empty-handed. The question now is how to distribute our charity funds.

The verse in *Devarim* (15:7) states: "If there will be a poor person of your family, in one of your cities, in your land which *Hashem* gave you, do not harden your heart, nor close your hand, from your brother who needs help." From this we learn that we are required to help relatives first, then people from our neighborhood, and then people who live in *Eretz Yisroel.* There are priorities within these categories:

Relatives

1. First, consider the needs of your parents. If your parents need funds, you must care for all of their needs first (*Chasam Sofer, Yoreh Deah,* 229). If you can afford to, it is better to support your parents from personal funds as you thus dem-

onstrate more honor to your parents. This level would apply also to your *Rebbaim*, who are considered your spiritual parents. A *Rebbe muvhak* is compared to a parent, whose needs are a priority (See *Ahavas Chesed,* 6:7). There is a difference if the funds are to support your *Rebbe*'s personal needs or for his institution. We are speaking here of his personal needs.

2. After parents, the priority is to support grandparents.

3. The next priority is older children who are independent (over the age of bar or bas mitzvah) (*Derech Emunah,* chap. 10). Even if you can afford to support them from your personal funds, you may use *maaser* funds.

4. Following are grandchildren (who are considered as children.)

5. Next are brothers and sisters.

6. Then come other relatives.

Your City

7. Neighbors [even non-learned ones.]

8. Others in the community

Israel

9. Those living in *Eretz Yisroel,* with *Yerushalayim* first.

10. Those in other areas in Israel

Other People

11. Those living outside of your community and outside of *Eretz Yisroel.*

You must also consider how urgent the need is and whether the needy individual is a Torah scholar. If one person needs food, while another needs only clothing, the obligation to provide food comes first, (*Shulchan Aruch*, 251:7).

A Torah scholar in need comes before others in need, even if he only needs money for clothing (ibid, 251:9). However, if your relative needs money for clothing, whereas a non-relative needs funds for food, even if the non-relative is a Torah scholar, the relative comes first (Some disagree. See ibid.)

■ Levels of Need

- If the local poor need clothing and the distant poor need food, the latter come first.
- If members of your household need clothing whereas the local poor need food, your household comes first (*Chasam Sofer, Yoreh Deah,* 231).

■ Excuses

Can one ever say, "Why should I give that poor person money? Why doesn't he get a job?"

The Chofetz Chaim said that there are situations wherein *Hashem* decrees poverty on a person and his efforts to find a job will not be successful (*Derech Sicha,* p. 554). Therefore, we should give him *tzedaka.*

Keep in mind that if you are sincerely interested in helping people find jobs, that is a great form of *tzedaka,* as we have mentioned.

The Torah (*Devarim* 16:11) describes who should participate in *Yom Tov* festivities stating: "You should rejoice before *Hashem*; you, your son, your daughter, your slave and your maidservant... the Levi, the convert, the widow and the orphan."

Rashi points out in commenting on this *posuk* that the Torah designates eight categories of people who ought to be included in celebrating our holidays. Four are members of your household: your children and those who work for you in your house. The other four are people who may not have the resources necessary to pay for the considerable expenses associated with a *Yom Tov*.

Rashi quotes two *midrashim* and further states that *Hashem* says: "Your four (the members of your household) correspond to My four (those who may be in need). If you gladden the hearts of My four, I will gladden the hearts of your four" (ibid).

■ **TWO PARTS**

The rewards for giving charity are divided into two:

1. The primary rewards for the *mitzvah* are in the world to come.

2. There are fringe benefits in this world based on how much you benefit the poor (*Ruach Chaim*, Avos 4:1)

STEP SEVEN

WHY ARE THESE THE PRIORITIES?

Based on the priorities listed above, the first *tzedaka*-giving question in our minds should be: "What are the needs of my relatives?" (*Ahavas Chesed* 2:19). To understand why the Torah obligates us to help our relatives first, we should study the fundamental verse "זה לעמת זה עשה האלקים" "*Hashem* made this opposite that," (*Koheles* 7:14), which means that everything and everyone is positioned in this world by *Hashem*'s profound plan so that they collaborate, cooperate and serve as challenges to each other. They thus assist each other to grow.

We are all granted the power of free-will (*Bechira*) to choose virtue and overcome challenges of wickedness. *Hashem* positioned every person in a family with various types of relatives and neighbors to encourage them and to challenge them. We are tested by others to see whether we will survive and strive to remain virtuous, grow in patience, kindness and humility, and develop and perfect ourselves.

Everyone around us in our orbit, so to speak, was placed there by *Hashem* for our benefit. Charity begins at home, with our family and relatives. They are our primary tests and opportunities for success in life. Difficult people and rough situations test us to rise to the occasion and to keep making the best choices in our service to *Hashem*.

The second concern should be to help our neighbors and friends. This is based on the principle of *Kol Yisroel Arayvim Zeh la'zeh* – all Jews are responsible for one another. When the question is between giving to a local poor person or to a Torah scholar from elsewhere, some say that the local poor are first, while others say the Torah scholars are first, for they help the world more with their merits (*Ahavas Chesed*, 6:7).

It is always important to support Torah study, namely Torah scholars and *yeshivos*, since Torah is the guidebook to our purpose in the world, and Torah study is the spiritual sustenance of the universe, without which it would not exist.

■ EXAMPLE

If a young person passes away suddenly and there is a great need to put together funds to support his family, the relatives and friends from his *shul* and neighborhood are obligated to help. All those who are able to give should participate. Whoever had some connection to the person should be approached first to contribute (*Derech Sicha*, 555).

■ THE PARADOX

Hashem has designed this system of "Give a tenth so that you will become wealthy" and He implements it. "The more you keep on giving, the more you get." But if you try to hang on to it, the more slippery it becomes.

■ A STORY ABOUT RELATIVES

There is a famous story of a *Rebbe* who came to a wealthy individual to raise funds for that person's needy relative. The man said, "I am only a distant relative." The *Rebbe* asked, "Do you pray daily?" "Yes, surely," was the reply. "What is the first blessing of *Shemoneh Esrei* about? We ask for Hashem's help in the merit of our *Avos*. But aren't they only distant relatives?!"

■ ALWAYS PRAY FOR HASHEM'S HELP

We begin with a prayer now, and regularly on an ongoing basis, that *Hashem* should help us to merit knowing how to give *tzedaka* properly, and that we should give generously to the right causes.

Pirkei Avos (1:2) teaches the purpose of life:

The world stands on three pillars:

• Torah study
• Prayer
• Acts of Kindness, which include giving charity.

STEP EIGHT

SUPPORTING TORAH STUDY

Which comes first? To support younger children whose Torah study is considered on a very pure level, because they are considered sin-free, or to support *kollel* scholars who are studying on a high level, training to render *halachic* decisions?

The *Igros Moshe* (*Yoreh Deah*, 3:94) explains that it depends on the greater need for now. We must develop scholars who can guide the community and teach Torah. If they are in need of support, we should provide for them first. But if they are cared for, we need to support the children who study in purity.

■ LEVELS OF STUDY

How do we choose between two higher-level learning institutions, one for *kollel* scholars who are learning at the highest level and the other for *kollel*-level beginners (or late starters). Which comes first? This may also depend on "the greater need for now" guideline. Additionally, the *Shulchan Aruch* (*Yoreh Deah*, 251:9) states that: "The one who is greater in wisdom should be supported first." Therefore, the institution for scholars learning at the highest level comes first.

■ A REASON

It has been explained that there is a spiritual ripple effect: the more we support the highest places of Torah study, the more inspiration and growth will flow to all other levels of Torah study as well (*Tuvecha Yabiu*, vol. 2:79)

Every level of Torah study is precious and entitled to support. The question is only which comes first.

■ FULL-TIME STUDY

Is it better for someone to sit and learn with support, at a *kollel*, or to get a job so as to be self-supporting and to continue to learn in his free time?

It is definitely proper for a person to accept support in order to learn full time (*Ramoh, Yoreh Deah*, 246:21). Our sages teach that it is sinful not to accept support when one can learn more with support. Those who think they know better are being misled by the wiles of the Evil Inclination to distract them from more Torah study (*Igros Moshe, Yoreh Deah*, 2:116).

■ SHARING

The Vilna Gaon was asked, "But doesn't it seem that such a person is studying Torah in order to receive reward?" "The answer," he says, "is the other way around. One who refuses to share a portion of his rewards of Torah study is demonstrating that he is only studying to receive rewards. Rather, his goal should be to serve *Hashem* at the highest level possible, which means to strive to study Torah all day long, as much as is possible. Those who support him will share in his great merits because they enable him to learn."

■ RETIRE EARLY?

The Chofetz Chaim speaks about one who is very wealthy and who has enough funds to support himself and his whole family for the rest of their lives. Should he retire early and join a *kollel*?

It depends on many factors, such as whether he will be able to manage studying Torah all day or only half a day. Additionally, if his intentions are to keep on working so that he may continue his donations to charity and *chesed*, and/or to provide jobs for needy Jews, which is an even better form of charity than merely giving them charity, then his continuing to work can be justified (*Mishna Brura, Orach Chaim* 231:8).

■ KOLLEL SUPPORT

What about supporting one's son or daughter who is studying Torah in *Yeshiva*/Seminary or in *kollel*?

If you can afford to support them on your own it is better to support them from personal funds. But if not, it is permissible to support them from *maaser* funds (*Teshuvos V'Hanhagos,* Vol. 1. p. 376). The Chofetz Chaim (*Ahavas Chesed*, 19:1), says it is a preferred use of *maaser* funds because it is a priority of assisting relatives.

However, the Chasam Sofer (*Yoreh Deah*, 231) says the parents must have had the intention to use *maaser* funds initially. If they first planned to use personal funds and now want to change to *maaser* funds, there are *halachic* questions.

The Chasam Sofer also recommends dividing the *maaser* funds to use half for others in need, and half for one's children.

This *halacha* is actually stated openly in *Shulchan Aruch, Yoreh Deah,* 251:3 where we have a list of priorities:
* To support older children is considered *tzedaka*:
  * To teach boys Torah
  * To guide daughters on the proper path
* To help parents is considered *tzedaka*.
* To help other relatives is considered *tzedaka*.

The same applies to the *mitzvah* of marrying off one's children; namely that *maaser* money may be used if necessary (ibid, p. 378).

■ LEVELS OF NEEDS

We have an additional guideline for assessing the priorities of four types of needs:

- Poverty
- Leprosy (healing illnesses)
- Blindness
- Childlessness

All these are considered urgent needs, but this is the order of these priorities (See *Tuvecha Yabiu,* 1:199).

DETERMINING MAASER

What can be considered maaser?
How should maaser be apportioned?

STEP NINE

WHAT CAN BE CONSIDERED MAASER?

The Ramoh (*Yoreh Deah*, 249:1), teaches that one who separates general *maaser* money should distribute that money to poor people. To avoid *halachic* complications, a person should ideally stipulate, initially, that he wants to utilize his *maaser* money for various other *mitzvos* as well (*Chofetz Chaim*).

One should not divert all his funds to *mitzvah* projects. He can distribute half for the poor and half for other *mitzvos* (*Chasam Sofer, Yoreh Deah*, 231). One who is learning these laws now who wishes to change from a previous method may need to first be *matir neder* in front of three people, according to some *poskim*.

Those *mitzvos* which one is obligated in as independent obligations, such as tzitzis, *tefilin*, mezuzah, *sukkah*, *esrog*, *matzah*, etc, should be bought with non-*maaser* funds. Similarly, one should not fulfill his personal *mitzvah* to buy or write a Sefer Torah with *maaser* money. However, if he is paying extra to help support a *sofer* who is needy, he can use *maaser* funds for the extra amount (*Hilchos Maaser Kesofim*, p. 138).

■ THE RULE

The general rule is that fixed obligations should come from your personal funds. Donations to charity are usually amounts you choose to give of your own volition.

■ FOR THE POOR

Tzedaka money should be used primarily for poor people and to support poor Torah students. One may not use *maaser* funds to buy an extra fancy *esrog* or other forms of *hidur mitzvah* (to beautify a *mitzvah*). Indeed, it is a *mitzvah* to beautify and honor *mitzvos*, but not at the expense of causing the poor to suffer neglect when the *maaser* money they are entitled to is withheld from them. (*Teshuvos V'Hanhagos*, vol. 2:392).

■ EXAMPLES OF MAASER (ALPHABETICAL ORDER)

Aliyos in Shul

If one purchases an *aliyah* and at that time had in mind to pay for the *aliyah* with *maaser* money, he can do so, because he is using the money for a discretionary *mitzvah*. If, however, he did not have in mind to pay for the *aliyah* with *maaser* funds, the payment is now considered his personal obligation, and personal obligations cannot be paid with *maaser* funds.

Baby Sitting

A woman who pays a babysitter to care for her children while she works can deduct the expense before figuring *maaser* (*Rav S.Z.* Auerbach, *Yeshurun* 15:148).

Building a Shul/Shul Enhancement

If the purpose for building a new *shul* is that a congregation has outgrown the building it now uses, *maaser* funds may be used. If a congregation is renting space and wishes to build a *shul*, *maaser* funds may be used. Where a community has no *shul* and wishes to build one, *maaser* funds may be used.

If the requested amount for a *shul* building fund is not a fixed obligation upon every *shul* member, it can be paid with *maaser* funds, even by the people who use the *shul*, because it is considered as a general donation.

Grandparents, who are asked by their children for money to pay for a building fund, may use their *maaser* funds for this, because it is not an obligation upon them.

What about building a fancier *shul* building, where none of the above situations apply? One should avoid using *maaser* funds if there are other more pressing needs, such as helping those who are ill or supporting those who are learning Torah. However, if a fancier *shul* will attract more people, it may be justified (*Teshuvos V'Hanhagos,* Vol. 1 – 386)

Burial

One may not use *maaser* funds to purchase a cemetery plot for oneself, even if it is in Israel (*Hilchos Maaser Kesofim,* p. 143). One may use *maaser* funds for those who need help with basic burial costs, whether for a family member, a stranger or for a donation to an organization that buries the needy.

Business Expenses

All clear-cut business expenses, such as uniforms, business travel, or a business meal may be deducted before figuring *maaser* (ibid).

Buying Ads

One may support a *Yeshiva* or organization by buying an ad in a yearbook or journal with *maaser* money (*Emes L'Yaakov,* 249:1).

Community Eruv

Maaser funds may be used for building and maintaining a community *eruv.*

Concerts/Productions

May *maaser* funds be used to pay for a ticket to a concert or production given to benefit poor people? The basic cost of the entertainment that you would pay should be deducted; the rest can be taken from *maaser* funds.

Domestic Help

A woman who works and hires household help may deduct the cost of that help from her *maaser* obligation. However, if the household worker performs jobs that the woman would not or does not do, then that amount should be taken into consideration when giving *maaser* (*Tzedakah U'Mishpat*, 5:8,35).

Finding Money

What if one finds money that he is *halachically* permitted to keep, such as a wallet with no name or identification in it? After he found the wallet a man comes up to him and says he has lost a wallet, and is able to say how much money was in the wallet. If the finder voluntarily decides to return the wallet to the owner, he must first give *maaser* money from his find (*Derech Sicha* p. 50).

Food Costs

Meals, etc, that one feeds the poor once in a while or on a regular basis can be deducted from *maaser* funds, (*Ahavas Chesed* 18:3), including money to buy kosher food for those who are not yet used to eating only kosher (Rav M. Feinstein, *ztl*, *Am HaTorah* 2:11). You can also use *maaser* money to pay for the *tzedaka* portion of a dinner or *melaveh malka* of a *tzedaka* institution; however, you should deduct the amount of the food costs, which you would have paid anyhow to have such a meal (ibid, and *Igros Moshe, C. M.* 2:58).

Goods and Services

If you donate goods to a charitable organization, whether new or used, you may deduct the value of the item as *maaser*. (If used, deduct the value at the time of donation, not the original cost of the item.)

What if you give of your time to a charitable organization? You may deduct the donated hours as *maaser* if you have a set fee per hour or a set fee for the service provided. For example, an electrician, a lawyer, a teacher, an accountant etc.

Hatzoloh/Saving Lives

One may use *maaser* funds for *hatzoloh*, for saving lives. This also includes funds used for preventing abortions.

You may use *maaser* funds to support an organization whose purpose is *Hatzoloh*.

Donations to hospitals can count as *maaser* if the money given is used for helping those who are ill.

One may deduct from *maaser* the transportation costs for a trip to donate blood for one who is seriously ill, since he is involved in saving lives.

Hiring Laborers

When you could hire a non-Jewish worker to perform a job at a cheaper rate, yet you choose to hire a Jew at a higher rate, the difference in price may be paid from your *maaser* funds, and you accomplish a great *mitzvah* (*Teshuvos V'Hanhagos,* vol 2, p 398).

Interest on Savings

An individual who has money earning interest in a savings account, and who then withdraws these funds in order to lend them to a poor person, the interest that the lender is forfeiting is deemed *tzedaka* and can be deducted from *maaser* funds.

Kiruv Organizations

May one use *maaser* funds to donate to a *kiruv* organization? *Kiruv* deals with four levels: food, clothing, *mitzvah* needs and education. To use *maaser* funds, it would be best if an organization deals with all four levels. If not, it would depend on the levels we have explained in general.

This is explained in *Igros Moshe* (*Yoreh Deah*, Vol. 2:240). "The primary *mitzvah* of *tzedaka* is to provide food and clothing, not in providing *mitzvah* items…" When the *Mishna* (*Avos* 1:12) teaches how to reach out to help others it states: "Be a disciple of Aaron. Love peace, pursue peace, love people and bring them close to the Torah." There are three stages before "bring them close."

Membership Dues

Are membership dues to national Jewish organizations/synagogue organizations considered as *maaser*? If the purpose of the dues is to support the organization, then yes. If one receives specific benefits for the payment, then no.

Mikvah

One may use *maaser* funds for building a *mikvah* (*Emes L'Yaakov*, 249:1). One cannot use *maaser* funds to pay for using a *mikvah* since this is a personal obligation.

Publications

One may use *maaser* funds to sponsor Torah publications that can be useful to the general public. When a poor Torah scholar is seeking funds to publish a scholarly work of *chiddushim*, the suggestion is to give the money to the scholar for his support, which he may then use at his discretion (*Derech Sicha*, p.553).

Purim and Pesach

Maos chitin (money given to the poor before *Pesach*) is definitely considered *maaser*. *Matanos Le'evyonim* (money given to the poor on *Purim*) can come from *maaser* funds when one gives more than the minimum amount, but the minimum amount is an independent obligation which should come from non-*maaser* funds. If you purchase *shalach monos* packages from an organization, the cost of the packages needed to fulfill the obligation (two per person) should not come from *maaser* funds.

Raffle Tickets

A raffle done as a fundraiser for *tzedaka* can be bought with *maaser* money if it is an unlimited raffle; that is, there is no limit to the number of tickets purchased, for it is considered giving regular charity. If the raffle has a limited number of tickets they will sell, and it is possible to figure out a value for each of the chances to win, *maaser* funds should not be used (*Igros Moshe, Orach Chaim* 4:76:2).

If you do win, you may keep the prize, but you should return to your *maaser* fund the original ticket price, so that you do not benefit personally from the *tzedaka* money. You are obligated to give *maaser* from the prize you win, and it is suggested that you give that *maaser* of the winnings back to the organization that sponsored the raffle.

Secular and non-Jewish Organizations

One may give to secular or non-Jewish charities in order to promote peace *darchei shalom*. It would depend if the money goes for causes that are in accordance with the Torah. For example, if a community center is open on *Shabbos*, it is forbidden to support it with any type of funds.

Seforim

If you buy *seforim* for yourself, you may not use *maaser* funds. You may use *maaser* funds for *seforim* you buy and donate, such as to a *shul*.

Shul Obligations

One should not pay *shul* membership dues or the cost of seats from *maaser* money, because the dues serve to pay for benefits which he gains (*Emes L'Yaakov, Yoreh Deah*, 249:134).

Summer Camps

It may be permissible to use *maaser* funds to pay for summer camp. The key here is whether the camp is only for enjoyment or whether it is mostly for Torah learning; that is, a summer program for children so that they will stay in a Torah/*mitzvah* environment.

Taxes

Are we expected to give a tenth from gross income or from the net amount?

Igros Moshe (*Yoreh Deah*, 1:143) explains that it depends on the type of tax:

Income tax should be deducted from gross income, because it is as if one did not make that income. The same applies to one's office overhead rental fee and the salaries of employees, which are not considered income. Business expenses such as buying uniforms for the staff may also be deducted before calculating profits (*Emes L'Yaakov* on *Yoreh Deah*, 249).

The same applies to taxes that one pays for homes which one owns to produce income. One may deduct those taxes first, before calculating the net profit from which to give *maaser*. However, you do not deduct the taxes you pay upon purchasing household items, goods for personal use and home taxes on your own dwelling before calculating the net profit from which to give *maaser*.

If one saves money on his taxes because of charity donations, that is his to keep (ibid). However, if one receives an independent tax refund, for large medical expenses or large real estate tax payments, for example, he should give *maaser* from it.

Tuition

Parents are personally responsible to provide their children with a proper Torah education. Therefore, they may not use *maaser* funds to pay for their children's tuition. This applies to both girls and boys (*Igros Moshe, Yoreh Deah*, Vol. 2, 113). *Rav Moshe Feinstein, ztl*, explains that since the law of the land requires every parent to send his daughter to school, a Jewish father is obligated to give his daughter a Torah education in order to eliminate the negative influences of a public school, where her belief in *Hashem* and her dedication to Torah and *mitzvos* are in great danger. Parents, therefore, cannot use *maaser* money to discharge what is a personal obligation. Some rabbanim state that one can deduct as *maaser* the amount of tuition paid by a parent which includes scholarships for other children in the school.

Tutoring

One may pay a *rebbe* from *maaser* funds to teach or tutor poor boys, and this is considered a great *mitzvah* (ibid, 2:19:2).

Visiting Israel

One may not use *maaser* funds to pay for a vacation trip to *Eretz Yisroel* or to visit relatives (*Rav* Shlomo Zalman Aurbach, *ztl, Kol HaTorah* 39:89).

STEP TEN

HOW SHOULD MAASER BE APPORTIONED?

Half of the *maaser* funds can be distributed to one's needy relatives. However, if parents need help and one is unable to assist them from regular funds, one should use even all of one's *maaser* funds for them if necessary (*Chasam Sofer, Yoreh Deah,* 229). Similarly, if another relative has an urgent need, one may give him all his *maaser* funds (*Derech Emunah,* 7:104).

The other 50% should be distributed to other causes.

■ LOAN FUND

The Chofetz Chaim suggests that a person should start a free-loan fund (*gemach*) with a third of one's *maaser* money. Once the fund is set up, you should continue to add to it until you have a revolving fund with enough funds to cover the loan needs of others who may approach you. You can also join with others and form a loan fund for the community, (*Ahavas Chesed,* 2:18:1).

■ OPPORTUNITY

If a wealthy person has a poor family living as tenants in one of his buildings, he is obligated to fulfill the *mitzvah* of *tzedaka* to help that needy family (*Derech Sicha,* p. 554).

■ MAASER AND SOME TAX CONSIDERATIONS

1. There are areas in business where the laws of *maaser* differ from business and personal costs that are reported on a tax return, e.g., entertainment. Under tax law, if one entertains a client at a restaurant he would only be entitled to deduct 50% of the total cost as a business deduction. For *maaser*, one may deduct only the amount of the bill that is greater than the payer's ordinary expense for food.

2. There are examples of income which are only partially taxed or not taxed at all, yet are fully subject to *maaser*. For example:
   1. Inheritance
   2. Alimony
   3. Social Security Benefits
   4. Monetary and non-monetary gifts (*seforim* and china received and sold)
   5. Workmen's compensation benefits
   6. Life insurance proceeds
   7. Damages received from lawsuits and accident proceeds in excess of actual costs incurred due to the accident
   8. Welfare payments received
   9. Food Stamps received
   10. Money received from fellowships, scholarships and *kollel*
   11. Municipal bond interest earned

3. Many *poskim* hold that there is no *maaser* obligation on all indirect income. For example:
   1. Medical insurance paid by one's employer (except when benefits are paid out and there is an actual benefit)
   2. Non-monetary gifts (free food)

3. Gifts or subsidies received where the use is restricted for a specific purpose

4. If a home equity loan is taken out by an individual, and he uses the proceeds for personal reasons, he may deduct the interest from his personal tax return but not as *maaser*.

5. If a person buys and sells securities throughout the year, showing a net gain from his transactions, he does not have to pay *maaser* on that gain, since he has not withdrawn any of the proceeds from the stock market to be used for something else. If he withdraws the proceeds from the market, he pays maaser on the gains. (*Rav* Tzvi Spitz and *Rav* Moshe Heinemann).

6. A person purchased a personal home twenty years ago for $80,000 and sold it for $380,000. The *maaser* liability is the difference between the gain and the total annual rate of inflation for the twenty years he owned the home (*Igros Moshe, Yoreh Deah* Vol. II, 114). For IRS purposes the owner pays no tax because of the $500,000 exclusion rule.

HOW TO GIVE AND
BECOME MORE GIVING

Higher levels of giving
Developing the desire
Why is giving an act that helps us achieve greatness?
The benefits of giving

STEP ELEVEN

HIGHER LEVELS OF GIVING

The Rambam (*Matnos Aniyim*, 10:7) defines eight levels of giving: The highest level of giving is preventing someone from falling into poverty. In this way you demonstrate that you love others as yourself since you enable the person to become self sufficient. This can be done in four ways:

a. By means of a gift,

b. With a loan. We learn this also in The Rambam "Laws of Loans" (1:1): The mitzvah to provide loans is greater than regular charity because there is less embarrassment.

c. Forming a partnership with those in need, or

d. Providing the person with a job in your firm, or finding him a job elsewhere. Included in this level are buying his merchandise, becoming his customer and also sending him other customers/clients.

The Sha"ch explains that of these four options the latter two are the most ideal, because there is no shame at all when a person earns his livelihood through his own hard work.

■ DOUBLE ANONYMITY

The second level of giving is to do so in a manner whereby you will not know the recipient and he does not know you.

Third best is when you know who the recipient is, but he does not know that it is from you.

The fourth best level of giving is when the needy person knows you are the donor, but you do not see him or know him, so that he has less shame.

Fifth best is when you both are aware of each other, but you give before he even approaches you to ask for help.

The sixth level of giving is that when you are approached you give a nice amount.

The seventh level is giving a smaller amount when a needy person approaches, but you give with a smile, an apology and a pleasant demeanor.

The eighth and lowest level of giving is to give directly to the recipient without a smile.

■ ADD WORDS

"One who gives a poor person even a small coin, is blessed with six great blessings from *Hashem*, but one who also provides words of encouragement, receives eleven additional blessings (a total of 17)" (*Baba Basra,* 9b). Thus, for kind words the giver receives almost twice as many blessings than for giving only money.

It is especially important to remember to offer kind words if the needy person refuses to accept the amount that you are offering to give. In that situation it is best to engage in a sincere conversation and hear the person out as to why he thinks you should give more, and then politely explain to him your position. You can and should always give your precious smile, kind, sincere words, a heartfelt *brocho*, some humor, compassion, a handshake, friendship, advice, and a pat on the back.

■ TOP QUALITY

When giving to the poor, *Rambam (Sefer Avoda, Isurei Mizbeach*, 7:11) teaches that you should subdue your evil inclination by expanding your giving to offer donations of the very best quality. This is derived from the episode in the Torah where *Hashem* accepts Hevel's offering when Hevel donated from his best sheep, while *Hashem* did not accept Cain's offering, since the quality of his offering was below par. In all matters that are for *Hashem's* honor, we should give of the best quality. Hence, one who feeds a hungry person should give the best and tastiest food, and one who gives clothing or any other item should give of the best, when possible.

The *Rama*, in the *Shulchan Aruch* (*Yoreh Deah* 249:13) says a person should never exalt himself with the charity he gives. If he does, not only does he forfeit all of the rewards for the mitzvah, but he will even be punished for his boasting.

STEP TWELVE

DEVELOPING THE DESIRE

What should we strive for in our giving? "Give, without your heart aching when you give" (*Devarim*, 15:10). Just as *Hashem* "Opens His hand and satiates the desire of all the living," (*Tehilim*, 145:16), so too, we should learn to be generous and give with joy. "You should be wholehearted with *Hashem*," (*Devarim*, 18:13). We should train ourselves to perform all *mitzvos* with heartfelt willingness.

How can we train ourselves to give with a smile, not only on our faces, but also with an inner joy?

We need to learn to truly accept the Talmudic principle of "Give a tenth so that you will become wealthy," (*Taanis* 9a – top line – "עשר בשביל שתתעשר"). Contrary to the seemingly obvious, giving will not cause you to have less. In fact, it guarantees that ultimately and inevitably you will have more. Our Sages derive this lesson from the Torah. The Prophet Malachi urges us to see it come true in our lives by trying it out. The verse in Malachi 3:10 says: "Please test Me with this, *Hashem* says…." (It is as if we are doing *Hashem* a favor!...)

With the proper Torah guidelines, when you start to give and keep it up, you will develop a new, closer relationship with *Hashem*. It is like thinking and saying, "I know that *Hashem* is always taking care of me, thus I am willing to give this money back to those whom *Hashem* designates."

■ KEEP IN MIND

When a poor person comes to your door, *Hashem* is at his right side (*Tehilim,* 109:31) and God will reward you greatly for helping him. "כי יעמוד לימין אביון"

■ REMEMBER

Remind yourself that no matter how little you have, there are others who have less. No matter how much you give, there are others who give more. Thus, give because *Hashem* instructs us to do so, and because it is the most successful way of living.

A chilling story that will help us develop our desire to always give is that of a poor woman who knocked on the door of a poor fellow who had a large family and few assets. The woman insisted that she needed some chicken for her family. The honest man began to explain that he did happen to have two chickens in his freezer for *Yom Tov,* but that he needed them for his own family.

She nevertheless insisted that she needed it. He thought it over quickly and decided that she may need it even more than he. He rushed off to his refrigerator to get the chicken she had requested. There he found his three-year-old son stuck in the unit, where he had been hiding while playing a game of hide and seek.

The father's mitzvah effort had revived his son just in time, for "*Tzedaka* saves from death" "צדקה תציל ממות" (*Mishlei,* 10:2 and 11:4).

A *mitzvah* is always worthwhile for its' own sake, not just for the rewards.

No matter where you work, what your job is and where you find yourself, you never know when a *mitzvah* opportunity may present itself. In every interaction you have with others, you have awesome choices to make.

You can decide to treat others in a positive manner, to make them feel important. When you act in a kind and compassionate way, people leave you feeling better and happier.

When you interact with someone on a business level, for instance, is there any reason to leave them feeling cold, unimportant and invisible? Why not display some warmth and treat them as someone who is created in *Hashem's* image?!

When you communicate your appreciation and respect for others in an enthusiastic and caring way, you are fulfilling many great *mitzvos* that are priorities of *tzedaka*.

There are many ways to show how much you care for others, but you should begin at the beginning; wherever you are, wherever you go, focus on helping one person as a start.

You are not expected to complete all of the work (to help everyone), but you are not exempt from helping as many as you can, (*Avos*, 2:16).

Rav Moshe Feinstein, *ztl,* always kept a large jar filled with quarters in his house. Before the rabbi left for a public affair, the *rebbitzen* would reach her hand into the jar and give her husband coins, so that he could give something to every solicitor he might meet. *Rav* Moshe never refused a request for *tzedaka*. Even if numerous children would solicit him for the same cause, he would give each of them a coin. He did this for *chinuch* purposes, to show them a good example, so that these children would learn not to refuse the requests of people when they grew older and were in a proper position to give.

■ MEASURE-FOR-MEASURE

"One who shuts his ears to avoid listening to the cries of the needy, when he calls out for help, he may also not be answered" (*Mishlei,* 21:13).

■ THE POWER OF CHARITY

Rabbi Judah said: "Great is charity in that it brings the redemption nearer." He also used to say: "Ten strong things have been created in the world. The rock is hard, but iron cleaves it. Iron is hard, but fire softens it. Fire is hard, but water quenches it. Water is strong, but the clouds bear it. Clouds are strong, but the body bears it. The body is strong, but fright crushes it. Fright is strong, but wine banishes it. Wine is strong, but death is stronger than all of these. However, charity saves from death, as it is written, 'Righteousness (tzedaka) delivers from death'" (Proverbs 10:2).

WHY IS GIVING AN ACT THAT HELPS US ACHIEVE GREATNESS?

When we give to others we emulate the ways of *Hashem*, the Greatest Giver. He created everything in abundance and He always keeps on giving to us. We were created in His image. Thus, we have the potential to give more to others and to enjoy the process.

Why is giving with a sincere, caring attitude and approach much greater than just giving? True giving is about touching lives. When you give in a caring way, you strengthen people's hopes and beliefs in themselves and in *Hashem*. You are helping them with their needs and touching them by your warmth and caring, from the essence of your soul. Everyone needs a connection with another person who sees them and their needs, and who treats them as a human being.

■ THREE SOURCES

"Greet everyone with a thoughtful, pleasant face" (*Avos*, 1:15).

"Be first to greet everyone" (ibid, 4:20).

"Greet everyone with joy" (ibid, 3:16).

The *Shulchan Aruch* combines the teachings of these three *Mishnayos* in one sentence (*Yoreh Deah*, 249:3) by stating: "One should give *tzedaka* as soon as possible with a thoughtful, pleasant face, with joy and with a happy heart."

Show others that you care about them. When you show that you cherish and appreciate them, they will be touched and feel treasured. *Hashem* created us with an inner potential to be a giver, as He is. Giving is the key to redemption (*Rambam, Laws of Giving,* Chap 10:1), since the more we give, the more we are living the way *Hashem* intended us to live. The more we help others, we are in a sense redeeming them. So too, measure-for-measure *Hashem* will do the same for us. You make a difference in the world by helping others, and you change yourself as well.

"אין ישראל נגאלין אלא בצדקה"

THE BENEFITS OF GIVING

The *sefer Hilchos Maaser Kesofim* (Chap. 27) lists the following as some of the benefits of giving *tzedaka*:
1. You gain wealth,
2. You will be saved from all harm,
3. You will develop a more powerful trust in *Hashem*.
4. One who does not seem to become wealthy should still re-alize that *Hashem* is granting him many benefits in many ways, and that the greatest benefits are the long-term re-wards of the World to Come.
5. Included in these blessings is the protection of one's assets.
6. One's prayers will be accepted more readily.
7. *Tzedaka* protects one from illness.
8. *Tzedaka* is a merit for having healthy children.

The power of *tzedaka* to save a person from death is well known, as it states in *Mishlei*: "Charity saves from death," (*Mishlei*, 10:2). On *Rosh Hashanah* and *Yom Kippur* we recite the phrase "*Tes-huva, Tefilla* and *Tzedaka* remove evil decrees"

The concept of "Give a tenth so that you will become wealthy" (*Taanis*, 9a) is both logical and a miraculous blessing from *Hash-em*. God established this world and built in to it both physical systems, such as the law of gravity, and spiritual systems, such as measure for measure. Everything we do produces results in the physical world and in its spiritual counterpart. "One *mitz-vah* leads to another *mitzvah*," (*Avos*, 4), is an example of such a systemized law. For every action we take there are physical and spiritual reactions.

■ LONG TERM

At times, one may give and give without noticing obvious results. However, *Hashem's* systems always function. There is no random chance in His world, although we may not understand or see the pattern. "Everything is in *Hashem's* hands" (*Brochos*, 33b). A properly planted seed generally grows, but the results may not be seen for a long while. In order for us to have the free-will to choose to give, *Hashem* doesn't make the benefits too obvious, but they are discernable when we study and practice the *mitzvah*.

■ EXCEPTIONS

One who feels that he is not receiving the benefits he expected may consider these possibilities:

- If his assets are not "clean" from all forms of theft, he may not become wealthy.
- If he does other things that may cause poverty, it may prevent the positive from being effective.
- *Hashem* has ways of providing benefits that are equivalent to wealth, and are even better. The Steipler Gaon, *ztl*, was once asked: "You have been a *sandek* so many times. Did it help you become wealthy?" (Being a *sandek* is a merit that can lead to wealth.) He responded: "For me, the definition of wealth is to publish many *seforim* and yes, I was meritorious to do so which is my great wealth."

■ ASK YOURSELF

- Are you giving as much as you should be giving?
- Are you following all the laws of proper giving?
- *Hashem* looks at the full picture of the world in a global, eternal way, to provide you with the ultimate benefits for the World to Come.
- *Hashem* sends benefits in disguise at times.

■ ACCIDENTAL CHARITY

This principle of gaining benefits from helping others goes so far that our Sages teach that even if someone lost some money which a poor person happens to find, Heavenly blessings will be forwarded to the ex-owner of the money, for the kindness that his money happens to provide (*Rashi, Parhsas Ki Seitzei, Dvarim,* 24:19).

■ WHEN IN DOUBT

Whenever I had a question on issues of *maaser* and I would ask my father, the Steipler Gaon, *ztl,* he would say, "Always be stringent and give more, for you will gain from it." (ibid).

Rav Chaim of Voloshin had a question as to whether he had to give a certain amount of *maaser* money. He decided to be lenient and not give the amount. Right after that his family lost some items. He calculated the amount of the loss and realized it was equal to the amount he was reluctant to give to *maaser*. He quickly gave the *maaser* and the items were subsequently found (*Keser Rosh,* 124).

■ PROTECTION

One who helps those who are needy is as one who invests in an insurance policy that can protect from all troubles (*Tuvecha Yabiu,* vol. 1:300).

A person stopped giving *maaser* to save some money, until he slipped and broke a leg. He eventually realized that the medical bills equaled to that amount which he thought he was saving (ibid, vol. 2: 306).

A collector of *tzedaka* has a greater *mitzvah* than one who merely gives, because the one who gives does so for himself. Someone who gets others to give does something for others rather than for himself. Someone who gives charity receives respect. Someone who collects from others may suffer humiliation, disappointment and rejection. Thus his rewards increase. "According to the difficulties, the rewards increase" (*Avos,* 5:23).

THE GIVING PLAN

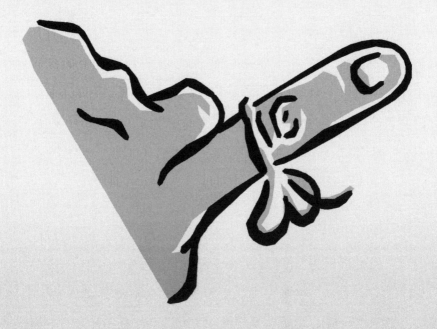

Give on a regular basis
Give tzedaka every day
General guidelines
Suggested priorities

STEP FIFTEEN

GIVE ON A REGULAR BASIS

It is better to give on a regular basis rather than randomly, even if one who gives randomly ends up giving as much as a tenth of his profits. By giving regularly your whole business (or every paycheck you receive) becomes a *mitzvah* enterprise. By designating a portion of all of your activities for *Hashem* you elevate all of your activities. (*Chofetz Chaim* in *Ahavas Chesed* 20:6, *Igros Moshe, Yoreh Deah*, 1:143).

The best time to give is upon receipt of income, whether daily, weekly, monthly or quarterly. This has been explained with the principle of "*Reishis*," give of your first, which we find in many places throughout the Torah, such as the "first of your grain," "first of your wool shearing," etc. If you write out other checks first, it may indicate your reluctance to fulfill this obligation. However, if you make out your *tzedaka* donations first, it is a demonstration of honor to *Hashem*, and that you consider Him to be your Senior partner in all of your business affairs (as well as for everything else in life). A consistent approach will make it easier for you, and it demonstrates your determination to do things correctly.

The first year when one establishes himself, one should give a tenth from the principal, if he has received a monetary gift or inheritance with which to begin. From then on, he gives a tenth from the profits (*Shulchan Aruch, Yoreh Deah*, 249).

■ Four Steps

In general, the Chofetz Chaim teaches four steps (*Ahavas Chesed,* 2:18:2) to simplify the process of giving *maaser* on a regular basis:

a. Decide and announce that your commitment to this program is *bli neder* (without a vow) so that you do not get into *halachic* questions if complications arise.

b. Use a ledger to keep track of all your incoming profits, as well as deducting your basic business expenses. Record also all that you give, including all the donations you give regularly – even the small amounts. (A suggestion that may make it easier is to set up a separate bank account for your *maaser*, into which you deposit a tenth of all the profits you earn. You can then give your *tzedaka* from this account.)

c. You should balance the account at least once a year.

d. When you balance your account, if you still owe to *maaser*, pay it as soon as possible. If you gave more, you may pay yourself back from incoming funds.

■ Consider

Link your charity giving so that it is a partner in your business. As you prosper, you will be giving more.

Choose a cause or causes you are committed to with a passion so that you are eager to fulfill the *mitzvah*.

Step Sixteen

Give Tzedaka Every Day

It is a good idea to place some charity money into a *pushka* box before every prayer [See *Yoreh Deah*, 249:14]. This *halacha* is taught twice in *Shulchan Aruch*, the first time in the laws of prayer, because it enhances our prayers. When you give before prayer, *Hashem* says, "You deserve to receive your requests, measure for measure, because you are helping others with their requests."

It is also mentioned a second time in *Hilchos Tzedaka* (*Shulchan Aruch, Yoreh Deah*, 249:14), because it is a higher form of giving when you demonstrate that you recognize *Hashem* as the Source of your prosperity, and that you want to utilize your money properly.

In addition to giving some charity every weekday, there are specific times that should be utilized for giving *tzedaka*, such as:

- Before prayer, as mentioned. Some give also during *Pesukei D'Zimra* when they say: "Wealth and glory comes from You and You rule over everything" (*Mishna Brura*, 92:36), in order to demonstrate that we are not just giving lip service, but realize that the money in our pockets is from *Hashem*.

- On Mondays and Thursdays (See *Sha"ch, Yoreh Deah*, 249:4).

- Before lighting *Shabbos* lights, to demonstrate that we want to help others also light up their lives, and that *Hashem* should do the same for us.

- On *Erev Rosh Chodesh* – The *Talmud* (*Beitza* 16a) says that a person's annual income is fixed by *Hashem* at *Rosh Hashana* time, for the entire year, but that there are some exceptions; money spent for *Shabbos, Yom Tov,* Torah study and *Rosh Chodesh.*

Rosh Chodesh is explained in *Shulchan Aruch Orach Chaim* (419): The Beis Yoseif teaches that *Rosh Chodesh* refers to tuition for Torah study which was paid at that time; the Bach suggests that it refers to *tzedaka* funds that are sent to help support Torah teachers. Others teach that it is funds for increased meals on *Rosh Chodesh.*

• It is suggested to increase charity giving on one's birthday, in gratitude to *Hashem* for the great gift of another year of life.

• A *chassan* and *kallah* should each give on the day of their wedding. Their parents should also give.

• Some have a custom before others leave on a trip to give them some money to distribute to charity at their destination, so that they become agents for a *mitzvah* cause. The traveler can also set aside some money, which he marks off with a *siman* to plan to give it, *bli neder,* to charity at his destination (*Kaf Hachaim,* 110:27).

■ SPECIAL THANKS

• If a person was fortunate to experience a miracle in his life he should –

1. Contribute charity to those who study Torah and say that it should be as a form of bringing a *korban Todah* at the *Beis Hamikdosh,* until it is rebuilt soon.

2. Say the *parsha* of the *Todah* offering.

3. Provide funds for some public needs in his hometown, and

4. Every year on that day spend some time thanking *Hashem*, rejoicing and relating *Hashem's* kindness (*Mishna Brura* 218:32).

- One should give extra charity to help atone for misdeeds (*Rambam, Teshuva* 2:4) such as if someone, *chas v'shalom*, desecrated the *Shabbos* (See *Orach Chaim* 334:26).

- There is a custom for women to put charity in a *pushka* before they engage in their three special *mitzvos:*
  1. Before separating *challah*
  2. Before going to the *mikvah*
  3. Before lighting candles for *Shabbos* or *YomTov* (*Ben Ish Chai, Parshas Lech Lecha*).

  A woman should also pray at that time for herself, her husband, her children and others. A person's prayers are more acceptable when they are linked with the performance of a *mitzvah*.

- During pregnancy a woman should increase her prayers and her charity (*Rabeinu Yonah, Igeres Hateshuva* 61).

- Before being treated for an illness. The *Sefer Zichron Beis Kelm* (p. 179) quotes the Alter of Kelm, who would bemoan the fact that physicians did not advise people to give charity as an aid in their healing process. He would advise to always give 18 cents (or $18.00, etc) to charity, to support people who study Torah (18 for *Chai* – life) before engaging in healing endeavors.

- If a person thinks that his time on this world may be coming to an end, let him focus on giving charity, for that may save him from death, and it can also save him from *Gehenom* (*Ahavas Chesed*, 3:3). (See also *Igros Moshe, Choshen Mishpot* 2:50, for how significant it is to donate to charity as atonement for sins when thinking of the possibility of leaving this world.)

■ GUIDELINES FOR A WILL

Someone had three sons, but two of them, sadly, did not follow the Torah way, thus there was a question as to the suggested way to divide the estate in such a situation.

Igros Moshe (Chosen Mishpot, 2:50) advises:

- He should donate most of his assets to charity.
- The son who is religious should be the executor of the estate.
- Each of the sons should get $1,000.00, as a basic amount.
- Each of the grandchildren should get a designated sum when and if they marry Jews.

■ PRIORITIES IN A WILL

For a couple without children, *Igros Moshe* (ibid, 2:49) advises:

- Set aside one fifth to distribute to one's siblings.
- Consider giving one third of the remaining 4/5th amount to Torah institutions.
- The remaining two thirds should be divided among relatives who study Torah or teach Torah full-time.
  - When dividing for this group –
    - First consider the ones with greater needs, due to family size and current sources of income.
    - Then consider those who grew up in your home. Give them more than the others, if the needs of all are equal.

These are some examples of "will" guidelines. For specific applications one should always consult a rabbinical authority.

■ MERIT FOR OTHERS

- It is customary to give charity at a funeral and also during the *shiva* – mourning period – at a house of mourning, as a merit for the deceased.
- It is customary to make a pledge to charity on *Yom Kippur* for the benefit of deceased relatives, as is mentioned in the *Yizkor* prayers (*Orach Chaim*, 621:6). The *Mishna Brura* explains that these donations are credited to the deceased, as we assume that had they been alive they would have participated in giving, or they would have desired to participate. In addition, if a child gives on behalf of his parents it is always helpful to the deceased, because children can provide merits for their parents. The Vilna Gaon says it is like sending care packages to those no longer with us.
- On the day of a *Yartzheit,* one should also give charity, and support Torah scholars as a means to elevate the souls of the departed ones.

■ SPECIAL MERITS

- There is a *segulah* for a couple that desires to have children to focus on the great *mitzvah* of *tzedaka* to always help poor people (*Ahavas Chesed*, 2:5). When you help others, *Hashem* will help you.
- Giving charity can also help as a *segulah* to find something one has lost or misplaced. By helping others find their needs, you will too.

- One who is struggling to understand a difficult Torah subject can give *tzedaka* and pray for Heavenly assistance (*Meil Tzedaka*, 1:276).

■ GIVE MORE

- Before each holiday, we should give more, so that the poor will be joyous on the holidays,
- During the ten days of repentance one should give more (See *Rambam, Teshuva* 3; 4), as we pray for a good new year.
- Before childbirth, as we pray for *Hashem's* blessings.
- Whenever a person merits celebrating a joyous occasion such as a *bris, vort,* wedding, *bar mitzvah,* etc.. One should always include poor people as honored guests so that they should also enjoy themselves with you. In addition, sending charity to them, if they are unable to be there, is recommended.
- It is customary to give charity on the day a three-year-old receives his first haircut. (*Radvaz,* 2:608)

■ PUSHKA

The *pushka* (*tzedaka* box) has been called "the little box that can save your life!"

It is suggested to keep *pushkas* (charity containers) in strategic places in one's home, to be able to take advantage of these opportunities. For example, keep one near the door, in your study, in the kitchen etc.

There are other suggestions of how to commit oneself to this *mitzvah* in a regular, concrete way. For example:

1. When going to a wedding, prepare yourself to give a dollar to every person who may be collecting at the affair. (You may end up giving out 5-6 dollars.) You will enjoy the affair more than ever, and you will also feel accomplished.
2. Offer a drink or snack to *meshulachim* (collectors) that come to your door, in addition to the donation you contribute.
3. Buy some food for the poor people who ask for money near the grocery store on Friday, if you are concerned that they may not manage money properly.

Tzedaka does not only apply to money. The Chofetz Chaim (*Ahavas Chesed*, 2:12) teaches that just as we should have a set time for Torah study daily, so too, we should do some *chesed* (kindness) daily. We can each choose some form of giving to specialize in, such as visiting the sick, comforting mourners, escorting the deceased, helping people get married, caring for guests, etc., which will allow us to express ourselves as created *b'tzelem Elokim* (in G-d's image).

In addition, whatever one's profession, one should also volunteer to do that, with some of his time, for *mitzvah* causes. For example, an accountant can do some work for a *Yeshiva* or a computer specialist can do computer work for a Torah or *mitzvah* cause. A physician can treat Torah scholars as a *mitzvah*.

The Chofetz Chaim once told a pharmacist, "I envy you for all of the life-saving you get to do." The man objected, "This is my occupation!" The Chofetz Chaim responded: "You should be thinking, 'I'm doing it for the sake of Heaven as a mitzvah endeavor,' but you also need to charge for your services, in order to be able to continue to serve in your capacity."

■ TRAINING PROGRAM

The Chofetz Chaim tells a story about someone who was going to work at a bank. At that time, banks had separate windows for withdrawals and deposits. He wanted to know at which of the two windows was a better choice to work at. The Chofetz Chaim said, "Work in the withdrawals window, as you will be giving out money all day. Even though it is not your money, you will get used to the idea of handing out money."

Yaakov Avinu said to *Hashem* (*Breishis,* 28:22), "For everything that You will give me, I will give a tenth to You."

The Ibn Ezra (on that verse) explains that in a symbolic sense that is why Yaakov's son Levi was set aside to be completely devoted to *Hashem*, as an approximate form of *maaser* for the children *Hashem* had given Yaakov. Although each of his children had set times for Torah study, prayer, devotion and activities of kindness, Levi was completely devoted to serving God.

Rav Moshe Feinstein, *ztl,* was famous for his teaching that a Jew should tithe not only his possessions, but should also to contribute 10% of his service time to serve worthwhile *mitzvah* causes.

■ FOUR "T's" OF GIVING
  • your Thinking
  • your Time
  • your Talents
  • your Treasures (such as money)

STEP SEVENTEEN

GENERAL GUIDELINES

The *tzedaka* laws discussed herein are complex in some areas. Thus, we urge that every individual should seek counsel with a competent Torah scholar regarding specific situations. These guidelines will help you know what questions to ask and what areas need clarification. The following are some summary guidelines which may be applicable.

At the beginning of the year (a person may choose his own cut-off date for this (*Shevet Halevi,* 5:133:3), a person should calculate his budget. Some suggest every year before *Rosh Hashana.* Others suggest twice a year or every month. Design a *tzedaka* plan based on your expected income. This includes how much you intend to give (20% which is the ideal amount, or 10% which is the amount an average person should give), how often you intend to give (once a month, weekly, or daily), and to which causes. Make a list of all the *tzedaka* causes that you want to support. Remember to first consider the needs of your family members, and then rank the others in order of importance.

Decide how much to give to each cause, leaving over a sum of money to be used as discretionary funds for miscellaneous causes.

Plan the timing of each donation. For example, if you have a brother who is poor and needs money for food. You allocate $1,200 of your *tzedaka* funds to go to him, deciding on whether to give him $100 at the beginning of every month or $600 before *Pesach* and *Succos.* Once you have an approximate schedule of when and to whom you will be giving, the process of giving *tzedaka* will become a part of your routine, and you will benefit more as a result.

This overall concept is explained by *Rav* Moshe Feinstein, *ztl* (*Dorash Moshe,* p. 52). A person should develop a great joy for giving *maaser* (a tenth) by understanding that this obligation causes the remaining 9/10 of your assets to become completely yours. Until you give the tenth, you owe it to the poor.

Hashem has provided you with extra in order that you distribute it to those who you are supposed to give it to. When you fulfill your obligation, you merit fully owning and deserving the remaining amount.

Never delay giving beyond the annual deadline. Every month or week is better, and the best way is to give daily.

■ GLOBAL PERSPECTIVE

What if people are collecting for an outside *yeshiva* in a community that has its own local, similar type of *yeshiva*?

Rav Chaim Brisker, *ztl,* gave an analogy to a wealthy businessman who had divisions of his company all over the world. Each branch had a manager who ran that division. Some of the managers would only focus on their branch, ignoring the others. But some of the divisions were run by the owner's sons. They had a different perspective. They were concerned about the success of all of the various divisions of the company. So too, as Jews we are children of *Hashem,* and we are concerned to support our Father's Torah institutions all over the world.

There is an incident, when *Rav* Moshe Feinstein, *ztl,* was collecting in Canada for his *yeshiva* in New York. Someone asked him, "Why are you collecting here? The institutions here are also struggling."

He answered: "My intention is only to collect from those who have already paid full tuition to the local institutions. Some Jews have been blessed with enough *maaser* funds to help us also in New York.

STEP EIGHTEEN

SUGGESTED PRIORITIES

For a net income of $100,000, the ideal is to give $20,000 to charity, so that you are giving 20%. But for the sake of simplifying our example we will take 10% of $100,000, which is $10,000. It would be divided as follows:

1. Two thousand will be designated for potential needy relatives, to be divided depending upon how many you have and the extent of their needs. (See page 57.)
2. Two thousand for community *Yeshivos* to be divided based on their needs and your connections to them. If the money in #1 will not be necessary for relatives, it will be added to this segment.
3. Two thousand should be set aside for the potential options of saving lives, helping people with jobs and helping people get married.
4. Two thousand for other forms of Torah study support.
5. Two thousand for giving daily *tzedaka* and to cover all the in-between cases such as the miscellaneous situations mentioned throughout the book.

The maximum amount of *Maaser* one should give is one-fifth of their net, which, in this example, would be $20,000 per year. $10,000 should be used for family-related causes and $10,000 should be dispersed to other causes, in the order of importance as was mentioned before.

For example, the $10,000 for family-related causes might be dispersed as follows, in this order, assuming the level of need is equal:

$1,500 to help your parents with their basic needs

$1,500 to help your in-laws.

$1,000 to support your *Rebbe* (See page 60.)

$1,000 for a married son learning in *kollel*

$500 for a daughter in seminary in Israel

$2,500 to help pay grandchildren's tuition

$1,000 to assist a brother learning in *kollel*

$500 to a sister to help with needs

$500 to a cousin living in Israel

- On the day of a *yahrzeit* one should consider giving $200 to your parents' favorite institution.

The $10,000 for other causes can be dispersed as follows:

$1,000 to local high school *yeshivos*

$1,000 to local elementary school *yeshivos*. If there are two local *yeshivos*, but one is where your children went, give that one $800 and the other one $200.

$1,000 to help save a life in your community

$1,000 for sick people in the community

$1,000 to a friend to help him start a business

$500 to a building fund for your synagogue (if it is not required of everyone)

$400 for synagogue dues

$500 for the community *mikvah* (building and usage)

$200 for funds for *Maos Chitim*, *Kaporos* and *Matonos l'evyonim*.

$500 for ads in support of your Alma Mater

$500 for raffle tickets or concerts in support of organizations in your community.

$500 to a *yeshiva* in Yerushalayim.

$1,000 to various *meshulachim* collecting for people and causes in *Eretz Yisroel* (door requests).

$1,000 to local organizations in United States (phone and mail requests)

If you add it up and see that we went over the suggested amount, there is an intended lesson – it pays to try to always give more.

May we merit *Hashem's* help to keep on giving properly to the right causes, and gain the results of God's blessings of prosperity. As we develop in helping each other, may we also merit *Hashem's* help for the complete redemption, speedily in our time.

Useful Tools for Tzedaka Giving

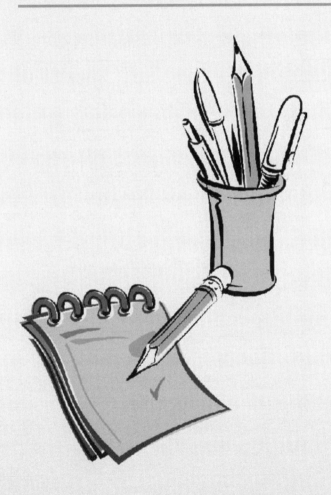

What follows are worksheet templates that you may use for keeping track of your *tzedaka*. The categories are generally organized so that they cover all the areas of *tzedaka* discussed in this book. There is a template for a worksheet that can be used for each week. There is also a template that can be used for the months of the year. You are encouraged to make copies of these worksheet templates. By utilizing these worksheets it should become easier to see how much *tzedaka* you are giving and to whom you are giving it.

■ WEEKLY TZEDAKA WORKSHEET

Week of   **to**

Helping Relatives

To	For	Amount
Total for Week		

Supporting Torah Study

To	For	Amount
Total for Week		

Helping Someone get Married

To	For	Amount
Total for Week		

Providing Assistance with Health/Saving Lives

To	For	Amount
Total for Week		

Supporting a Synagogue

To	For	Amount
Total for Week		

Door and Phone Requests

To	For	Amount
Total for Week		

Eretz Yisroel

To	For	Amount
Total for Week		

Daily Giving/Pushkas

To	For	Amount
Total for Week		

Miscellaneous Other Categories

To	For	Amount
Total for Week		

Goods and Services Donated

To	For	Amount
Total for Week		

Notes: _____

_____

_____

_____

_____

_____

_____

■ MONTHLY TZEDAKA WORKSHEET

Month of

Helping Relatives

Week #1	
Week #2	
Week #3	
Week #4	
Week #5	
Total for Month	

Supporting Torah Study

Week #1	
Week #2	
Week #3	
Week #4	
Week #5	
Total for Month	

Helping Someone get Married

Week #1	
Week #2	
Week #3	
Week #4	
Week #5	
Total for Month	

Providing Assistance with Health/Saving Lives

Week #1	
Week #2	
Week #3	
Week #4	
Week #5	
Total for Month	

Supporting a Synagogue

Week #1	
Week #2	
Week #3	
Week #4	
Week #5	
Total for Month	

Door and Phone Requests

Week #1	
Week #2	
Week #3	
Week #4	
Week #5	
Total for Month	

Eretz Yisroel

Week #1	
Week #2	
Week #3	
Week #4	
Week #5	
Total for Month	

Daily Giving/Pushkas

Week #1	
Week #2	
Week #3	
Week #4	
Week #5	
Total for Month	

Miscellaneous Other Categories

Week #1	
Week #2	
Week #3	
Week #4	
Week #5	
Total for Month	

Goods and Services Donated

Week #1	
Week #2	
Week #3	
Week #4	
Week #5	
Total for Month	

Grand $ Total for Month:

Running $ Total for Year:

Running Total Hours for Year:

TOPICAL INDEX

DEDICATION PAGES

Just as the twenty-two letters of the Hebrew alphabet form a foundation for the Torah, the twenty-two families who sponsored the following dedication pages formed the foundation for the dissemination of this *sefer*. Thanks to their contributions, almost 8000 copies of this *sefer* will be printed and distributed to every Orthodox synagogue across the country, as well as to all *Yeshiva* high schools and other organizations. We are grateful for their participation and wish them that they may go *"m'chayil el chayil."*

Tizku l'mitzvos.

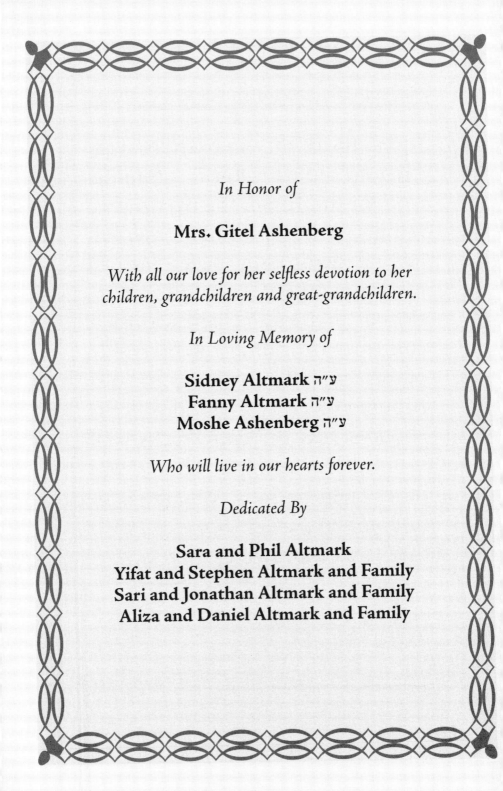

In Honor of

Mrs. Gitel Ashenberg

With all our love for her selfless devotion to her children, grandchildren and great-grandchildren.

In Loving Memory of

Sidney Altmark ע״ה
Fanny Altmark ע״ה
Moshe Ashenberg ע״ה

Who will live in our hearts forever.

Dedicated By

**Sara and Phil Altmark
Yifat and Stephen Altmark and Family
Sari and Jonathan Altmark and Family
Aliza and Daniel Altmark and Family**

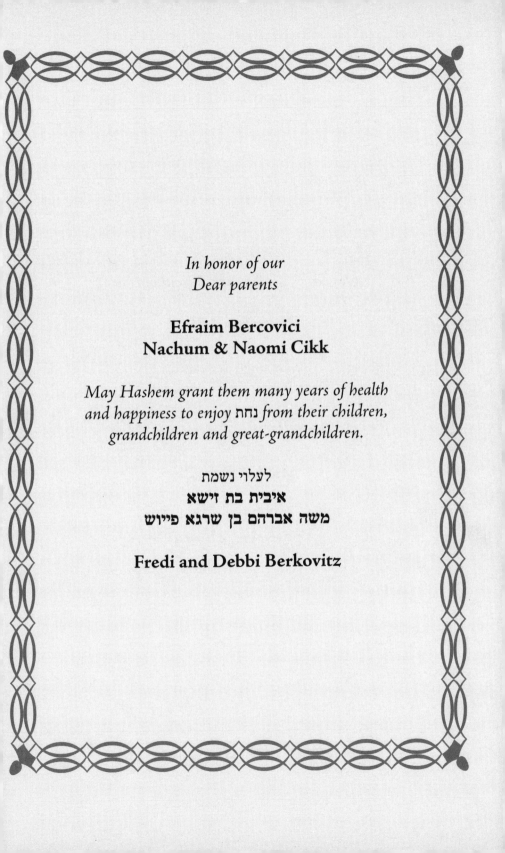

In honor of our
Dear parents

Efraim Bercovici
Nachum & Naomi Cikk

May Hashem grant them many years of health
and happiness to enjoy נחת *from their children,*
grandchildren and great-grandchildren.

לעלוי נשמת
איבית בת זישא
משה אברהם בן שרגא פייוש

Fredi and Debbi Berkovitz

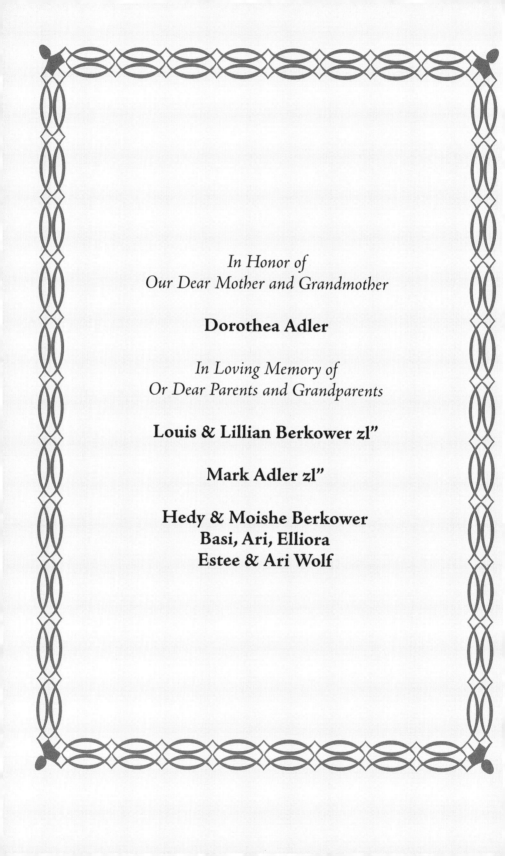

In Honor of
Our Dear Mother and Grandmother

Dorothea Adler

In Loving Memory of
Or Dear Parents and Grandparents

Louis & Lillian Berkower zl"

Mark Adler zl"

Hedy & Moishe Berkower
Basi, Ari, Elliora
Estee & Ari Wolf

DEDICATED BY

Cipora and Max Brandsdorfer

In loving memory of
Alexander Figula
ישראל בן מאיר מרדכי ז״ל

A valiant survivor of the Holocaust
From the original settlers of modern Meiron
Raised a beautiful Torah mishpacha in America
Lived to see three generations of Torah nachas.
ת.נ.צ.ב.ה.

In loving memory of
Meir and Molly Brandsdorfer
שלמה מאיר בן יהושע ז״ל
מלכה בת מרדכי ז״ל

From the original Bobover families in America
From a great line of Sanzer Chasidim
They survived the horrors of Aushwitz and Siberia
To persevere in their commitment to yiddishkeit
And raised a family dedicated to Hashem and His Torah.
ת.נ.צ.ב.ה.

DEDICATED IN MEMORY OF OUR
GRANDPARENTS AND PARENTS:

Miriam and Max Leibesfeld

Lena and Nathan Bromberg

Pauline and Hyman Rosa

Jenny and Albert Salitel

Hannah and Sidney Bromberg

Max Rosa

*It is with humble gratitude to Hashem that we
enjoy this Opportunity to participate as
Sponsors of this wonderful Torah Publication
Priorities in Tzedaka: The Art of Giving,*

In Honor of our dear beloved parents:
Toby & Joe Feder
-and-
Eve & Jack Weinblatt

*They've thus far led our family for nine decades with
ceaseless examples of love, dedication and service to
B'nai Yisrael, Eretz Yisrael and Am Yisrael in each of
the many communities that were fortunate to have them
as residents. They have given and continue to give their
time, effort, money, leadership and devotion to their
Shuls and to innumerable Communal, National and
International Organizations dedicated to B'nai Yisrael.*

*This much needed guide to Tzedaka is a publication
that we are proud to dedicate in their honor*
כל שרוח הבריות נוחה הימנו רוח המקום נוחה הימנו (פרקי אבות)
*"When one is pleasing and pleasant to others,
Hashem is pleased with them."*
*May Hashem grant them many more pleasant,
healthy and good years with their loving family.*

MINDY & SAUL FEDER, children and grandchildren

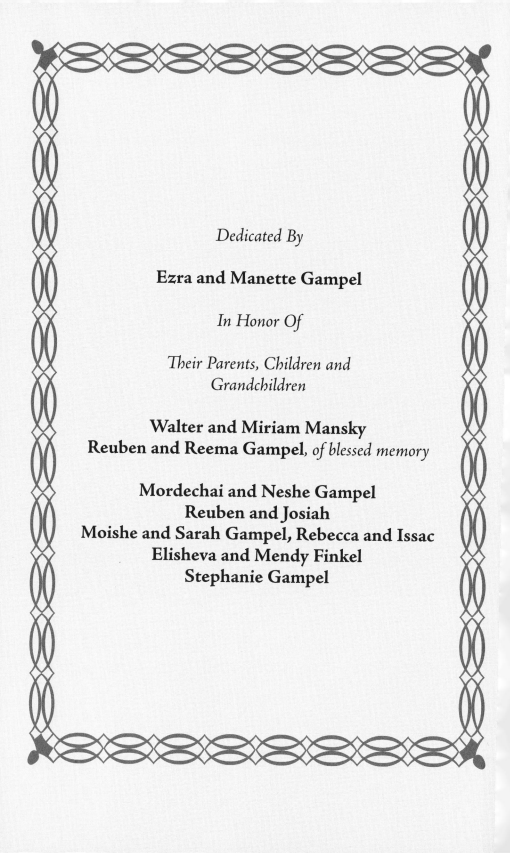

Dedicated By

Ezra and Manette Gampel

In Honor Of

Their Parents, Children and
Grandchildren

Walter and Miriam Mansky
Reuben and Reema Gampel, *of blessed memory*

Mordechai and Neshe Gampel
Reuben and Josiah
Moishe and Sarah Gampel, Rebecca and Issac
Elisheva and Mendy Finkel
Stephanie Gampel

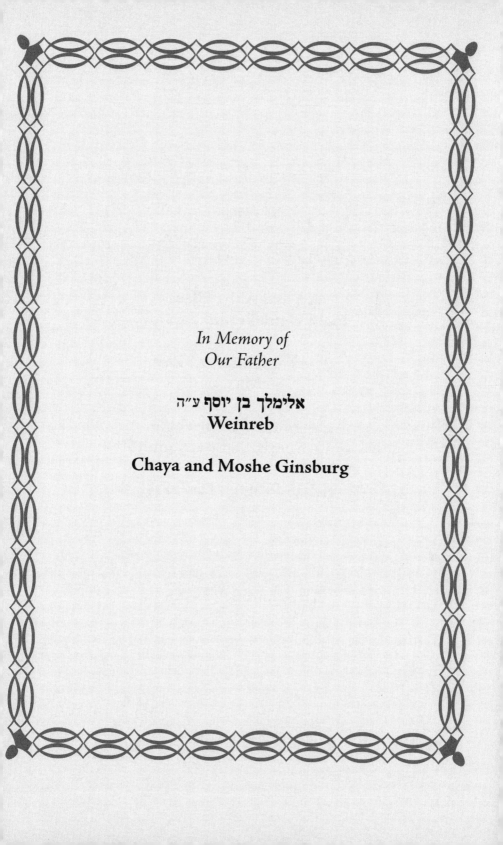

In Memory of
Our Father

אלימלך בן יוסף ע״ה
Weinreb

Chaya and Moshe Ginsburg

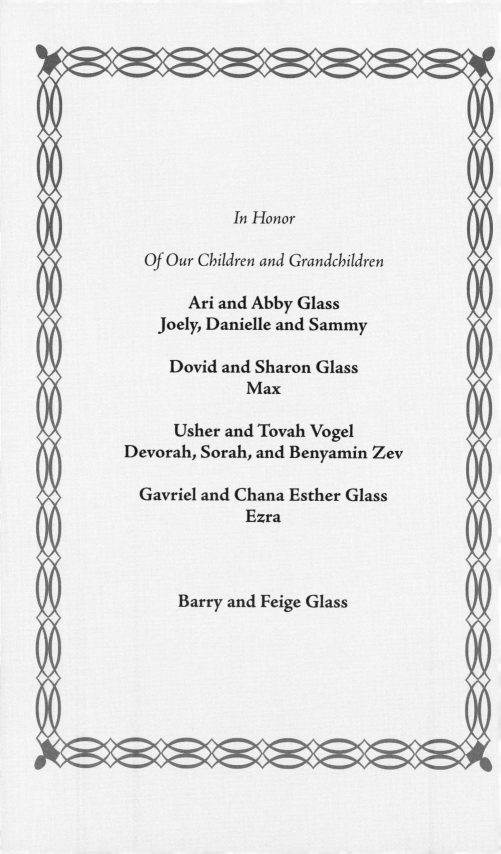

In Honor

Of Our Children and Grandchildren

Ari and Abby Glass
Joely, Danielle and Sammy

Dovid and Sharon Glass
Max

Usher and Tovah Vogel
Devorah, Sorah, and Benyamin Zev

Gavriel and Chana Esther Glass
Ezra

Barry and Feige Glass

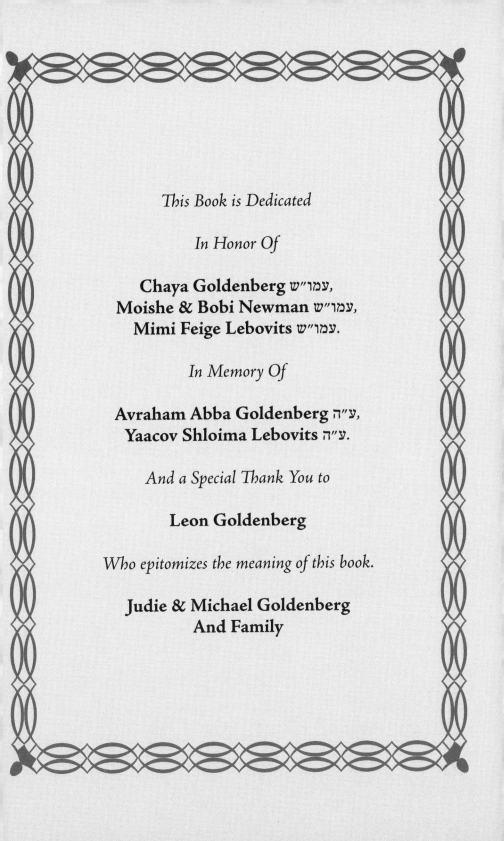

This Book is Dedicated

In Honor Of

Chaya Goldenberg עמו״ש,
Moishe & Bobi Newman עמו״ש,
Mimi Feige Lebovits עמו״ש.

In Memory Of

Avraham Abba Goldenberg ע״ה,
Yaacov Shloima Lebovits ע״ה.

And a Special Thank You to

Leon Goldenberg

Who epitomizes the meaning of this book.

**Judie & Michael Goldenberg
And Family**

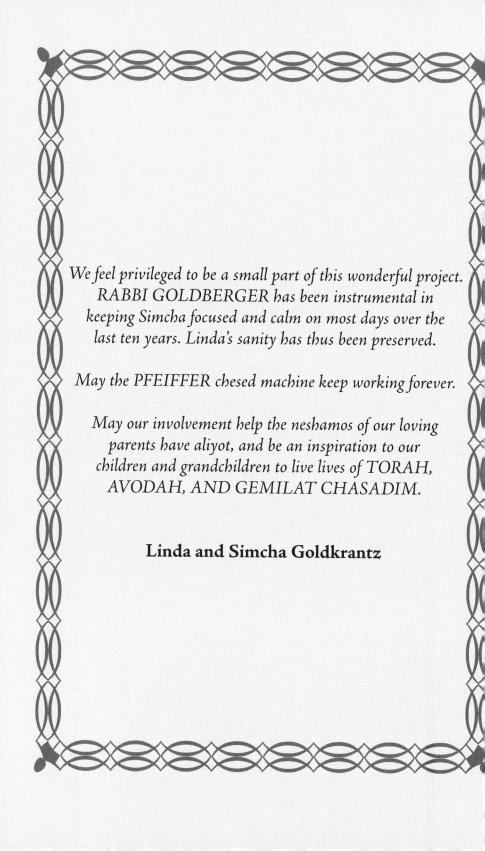

We feel privileged to be a small part of this wonderful project. RABBI GOLDBERGER has been instrumental in keeping Simcha focused and calm on most days over the last ten years. Linda's sanity has thus been preserved.

May the PFEIFFER chesed machine keep working forever.

May our involvement help the neshamos of our loving parents have aliyot, and be an inspiration to our children and grandchildren to live lives of TORAH, AVODAH, AND GEMILAT CHASADIM.

Linda and Simcha Goldkrantz

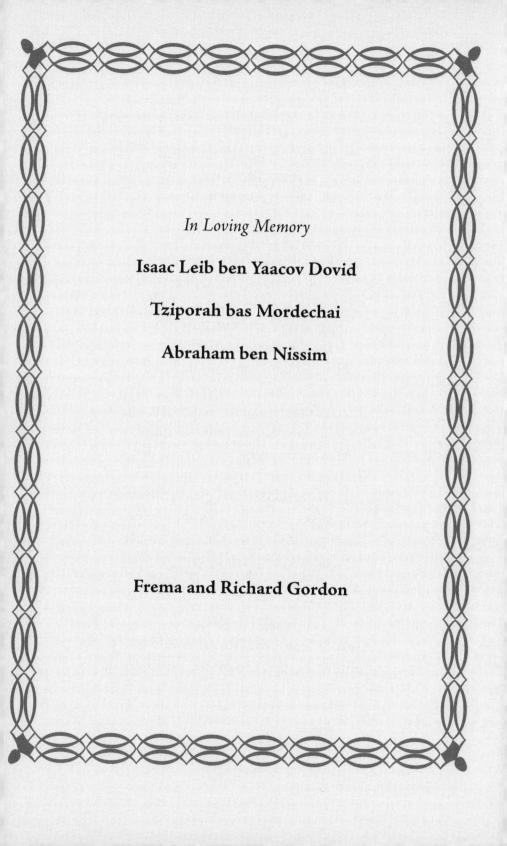

In Loving Memory

Isaac Leib ben Yaacov Dovid

Tziporah bas Mordechai

Abraham ben Nissim

Frema and Richard Gordon

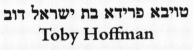

טויבא פרידא בת ישראל דוב
Toby Hoffman
ג׳ אייר תשס״ד

She escaped from the horrors of
The labor and death camps.
A young girl all alone,
All she had was her faith in Hashem.
She married and raised two sons
In the derech of Hashem.
Her two daughters-in-law called
Her "ma" and meant it.
The door to her home was open to all.
Her smile, kind words, and charitable acts
Were felt by everyone who met her.
She was an inspiration to her husband,
Children, grandchildren and great grandchildren
Who follow in her footsteps by having a
Shem tov and a strong sense of family.
She is still missed by everyone
Each and every day.

Josef Hoffman
Alan & Leah Hoffman and Family
David & Cathy Hoffman and Family

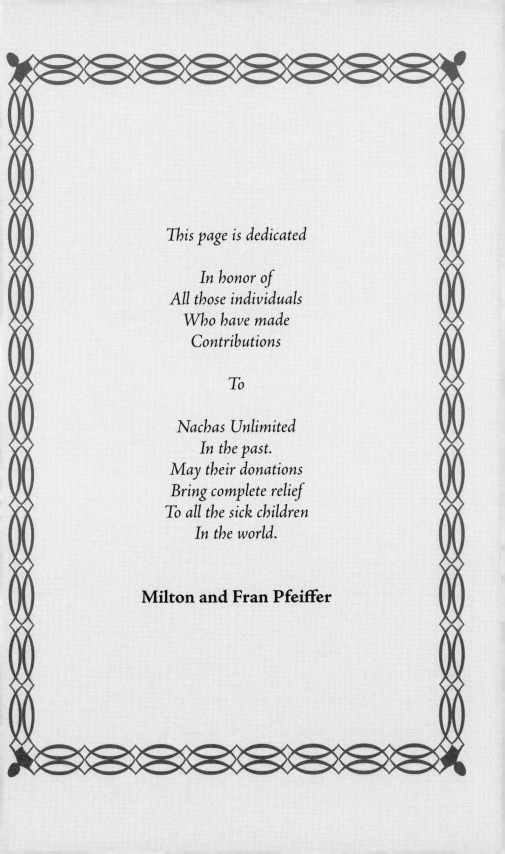

This page is dedicated

In honor of
All those individuals
Who have made
Contributions

To

Nachas Unlimited
In the past.
May their donations
Bring complete relief
To all the sick children
In the world.

Milton and Fran Pfeiffer

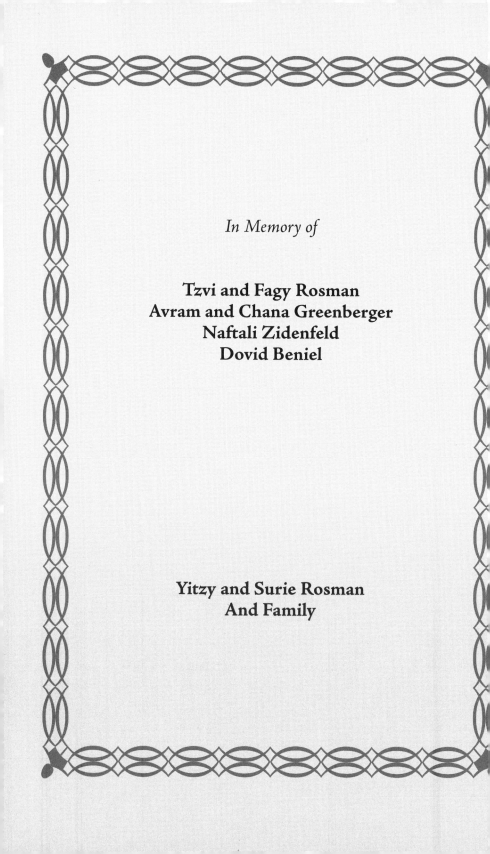

In Memory of

Tzvi and Fagy Rosman
Avram and Chana Greenberger
Naftali Zidenfeld
Dovid Beniel

Yitzy and Surie Rosman
And Family

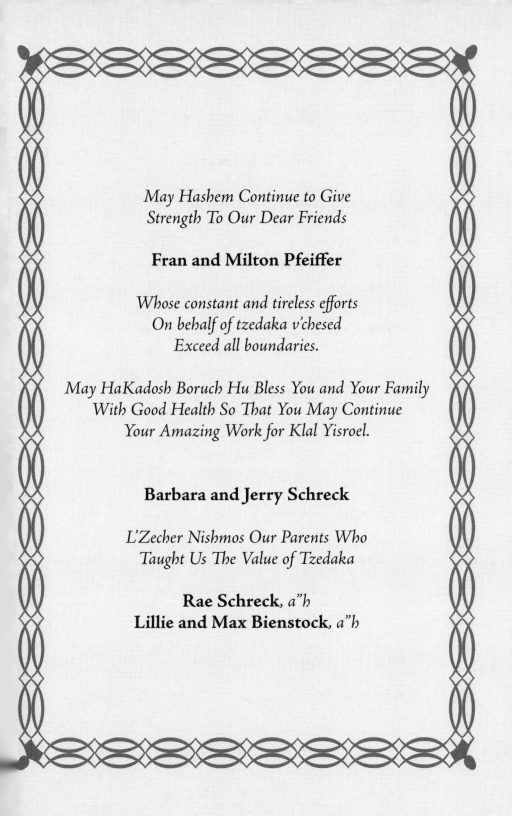

May Hashem Continue to Give
Strength To Our Dear Friends

Fran and Milton Pfeiffer

Whose constant and tireless efforts
On behalf of tzedaka v'chesed
Exceed all boundaries.

May HaKadosh Boruch Hu Bless You and Your Family
With Good Health So That You May Continue
Your Amazing Work for Klal Yisroel.

Barbara and Jerry Schreck

L'Zecher Nishmos Our Parents Who
Taught Us The Value of Tzedaka

Rae Schreck, *a"h*
Lillie and Max Bienstock, *a"h*

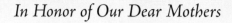

In Honor of Our Dear Mothers

Goldie Schwartz
&
Marlow Greene

You have given us the priceless gifts of being loving,
Gracious, embracing, happy strong mothers.
We take these precious gems with us to raise
Our families and continue your legacies.
Thank you for all the hours you spent making
Decisions for us, putting our needs first, and
You going without. All the things a child
Doesn't realize what a "Mommy" does.

May We Your Children,
Grandchildren and
Great Grandchildren

Bring you wonderful yiddish nachas. May we all do Great
things in your zechus and along with future Generations.
Let all our footsteps together follow the Derech of Hashem.

So Much Love
Heidi and Steven

Breezy & Eli	**Shloymie, Andy, Bennett**
Spencer & Aurora	**Gary & Shayna**

In Loving Memory

Our Matriarch
Our Savta

Bella Eitan

Holocaust Survivor and Thriver
Whose Emunah never ebbed
Who was Zocheh to love and teach to the third generation.

From her crowning glory, her beloved great grandchildren.

Sarnia Aliza
Liana Ykara
Chaim Simcha
Tova Leah
Aharon Ze'ev (Daniel)
Esther Devorah
Aharon Ze'ev (Zevy)
Yakov Yehoshua
Bentzion
Chaim Eitan

And their parents, her grandchildren

Yolanda and Sam
Susan and Eddie
Ariella
Shuster

This ספר *on* צדקה *is dedicated to our parents*

יוסף שמואל בן יהודה הכהן ע"ה
רבקה בת יהושע שמחה ע"ה
יצחק נתן בן יהושע
ח"ה רויזא בת ישעיה ע"ה

After surviving the Holocaust in Europe they came to America to start new lives. Our parents taught us that צדקה *was always to be given with kindness and compassion. Even in the years when earning a living was difficult, their message to us was that if someone is in need, give something and be happy that you have given.*

We are indebted to our parents for having instilled in us the spirit of this great מצוה*. We hope to keep their legacy alive by showing our children and grandchildren the spirit of always giving.*

Sheldon and Sabina Silbiger

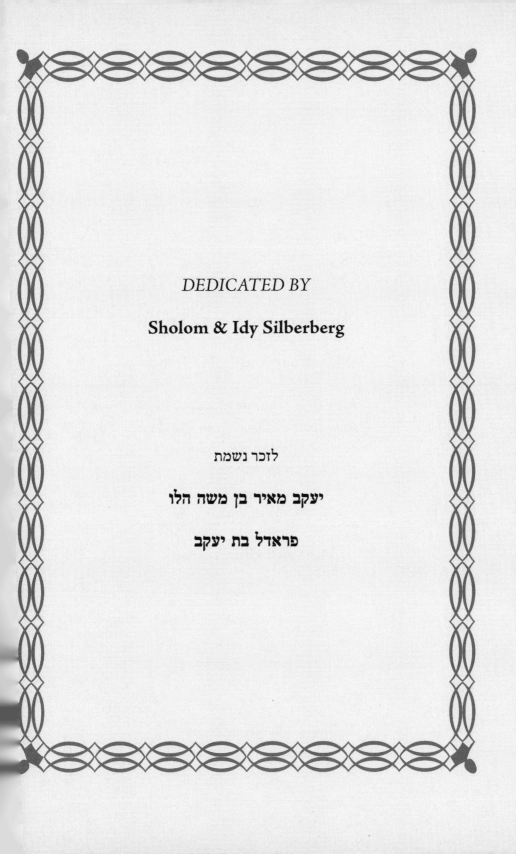

DEDICATED BY

Sholom & Idy Silberberg

לזכר נשמת

יעקב מאיר בן משה הלוי

פראדל בת יעקב

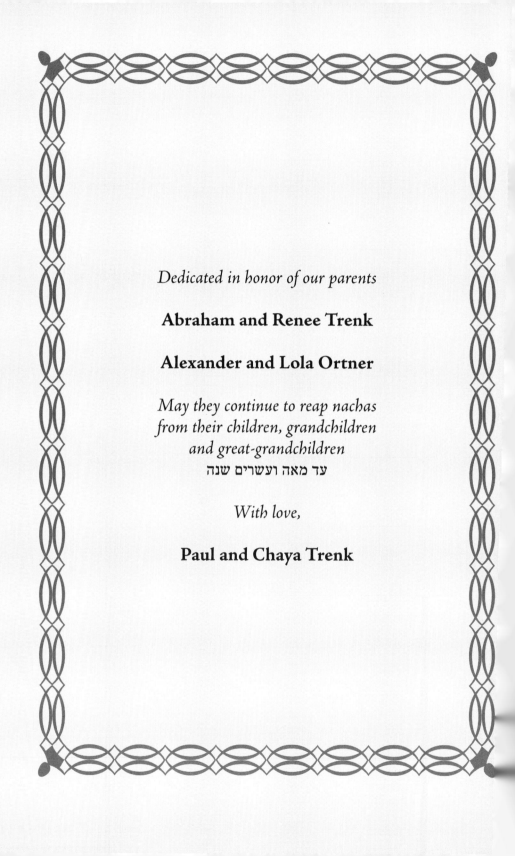

Dedicated in honor of our parents

Abraham and Renee Trenk

Alexander and Lola Ortner

*May they continue to reap nachas
from their children, grandchildren
and great-grandchildren*
עד מאה ועשרים שנה

With love,

Paul and Chaya Trenk

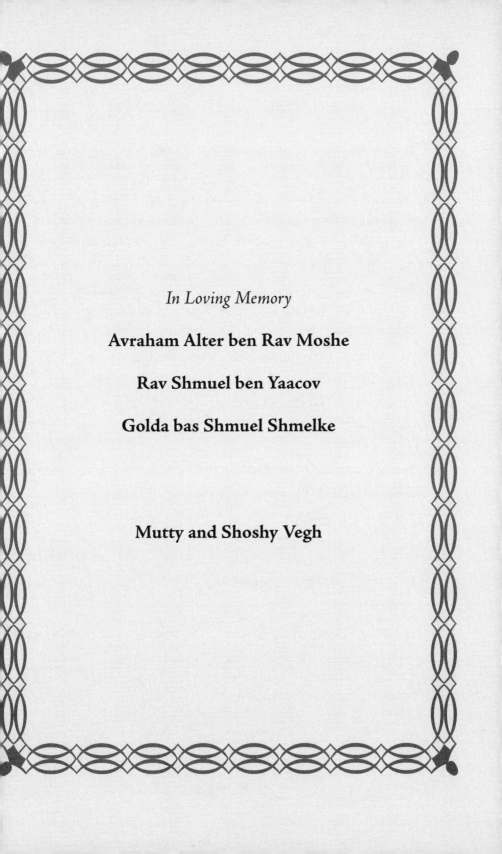

In Loving Memory

Avraham Alter ben Rav Moshe

Rav Shmuel ben Yaacov

Golda bas Shmuel Shmelke

Mutty and Shoshy Vegh

Author's Biography

Rabbi Moshe Goldberger is associated with the Yeshiva of Staten Island. He studied under both *Rav* Moshe Feinstein, *ztl,* and (*Le'Havdil Bein chaim L'Chaim*) his son, *Rav* Reuven Feinstein, *Shlita.* He also studied with *Rav* Avigdor Miller, *ztl.*

He is the author of over 15 books and 100 booklets and has produced hundreds of tapes on a variety of Jewish topics. He delivers a morning *Daf Yomi Shiur* in the Agudah of Edison, New Jersey, an evening *Daf Yomi Shiur* in Congregation Agudath Shomrei Hadas of Staten Island and a *Navi Shiur* in the Kollel Baal HaBatim in Willowbrook, Staten Island.

He lives with his family in the Pleasant Plains section of Staten Island and can be reached at 718-948-2548 or by email at rabbig@sakar.com.

• For consultations regarding individualized Tzedaka prioritizations please call 1-718-948-2548.
• For Tax guidance please call 1-718-761-8908.

NOW MAY BE A GOOD TIME FOR A GEM OF TORAH STUDY.
WWW.GEMSOFTORAH.COM